'An important compilation of transnational practice based on the collective perspectives of practitioners, local community leaders and academics on the field of toddlers' health and wellbeing. Pertinent current issues around disadvantage are confronted and reflective practical activities are proposed in a constant effort to meet universal needs and improve toddlers' lives.'

— Dr Paty Paliokosta, Senior Lecturer in Inclusive Education, Kingston University, London

'A fantastic read! An in-depth insight into what really attributes to the wellbeing of toddlers. It is powerful how each chapter with the 4 pedagogical characteristics offers information on legislation, proven research and an opportunity to reflect on your own setting using direct focus points offering further reading. It highlights areas to consider, comparisons are relevant and thought provoking and it enables the reader to test their own knowledge and settings paradigms. As a very experienced leader I still found this book refreshingly unique and a powerful tool.'

— Hazel Moody, Director, Advantage Day Nursery

'*Supporting Toddlers' Wellbeing in Early Years Settings* will prove valuable to all those working in the early years sector, and is an accessible and user-friendly resource that promotes increased professional responsibility. Theoretical underpinning and the use of case studies, activities and links to observed practice, provide thought-provoking material which recognises the importance of children's wellbeing. Emphasis is placed on the importance of reflection to question values and beliefs and to continually evaluate and challenge practice. This book aims to support inspirational practice that will enhance positive learning opportunities for all early years children.'

— Soraya Goni, Award Leader Higher Education Childhood Studies, Kirklees College

JUL - - 2018

SUPPORTING TODDLERS' WELLBEING IN EARLY YEARS SETTINGS

of related interest

Promoting Young Children's Emotional Health and Wellbeing
A Practical Guide for Professionals and Parents
Sonia Mainstone-Cotton
ISBN 978 1 78592 054 7
eISBN 978 1 78450 311 6

Helping Children Develop a Positive Relationship with Food
A Practical Guide for Early Years Professionals
Jo Cormack
ISBN 978 1 78592 208 4
eISBN 978 1 78450 486 1

Learning through Movement and Active Play in the Early Years
A Practical Resource for Professionals and Teachers
Tania Swift
ISBN 978 1 78592 085 1
eISBN 978 1 78450 346 8

Nurturing Personal, Social and Emotional Development in Early Childhood
A Practical Guide to Understanding Brain Development and Young Children's Behaviour
Debbie Garvey
Foreword by Dr Suzanne Zeedyk
ISBN 978 1 78592 223 7
eISBN 978 1 78450 500 4

School Readiness and the Characteristics of Effective Learning
The Essential Guide for Early Years Practitioners
Tamsin Grimmer
ISBN 978 1 78592 175 9
eISBN 978 1 78450 446 5

Child Protection in the Early Years
A Practical Guide
Eunice Lumsden
ISBN 978 1 78592 265 7
eISBN 978 1 78450 555 4

SUPPORTING TODDLERS' WELLBEING IN EARLY YEARS SETTINGS

of related interest

Promoting Young Children's Emotional Health and Wellbeing
A Practical Guide for Professionals and Parents
Sonia Mainstone-Cotton
ISBN 978 1 78592 054 7
eISBN 978 1 78450 311 6

Helping Children Develop a Positive Relationship with Food
A Practical Guide for Early Years Professionals
Jo Cormack
ISBN 978 1 78592 208 4
eISBN 978 1 78450 486 1

Learning through Movement and Active Play in the Early Years
A Practical Resource for Professionals and Teachers
Tania Swift
ISBN 978 1 78592 085 1
eISBN 978 1 78450 346 8

Nurturing Personal, Social and Emotional Development in Early Childhood
A Practical Guide to Understanding Brain Development and Young Children's Behaviour
Debbie Garvey
Foreword by Dr Suzanne Zeedyk
ISBN 978 1 78592 223 7
eISBN 978 1 78450 500 4

School Readiness and the Characteristics of Effective Learning
The Essential Guide for Early Years Practitioners
Tamsin Grimmer
ISBN 978 1 78592 175 9
eISBN 978 1 78450 446 5

Child Protection in the Early Years
A Practical Guide
Eunice Lumsden
ISBN 978 1 78592 265 7
eISBN 978 1 78450 555 4

SUPPORTING TODDLERS' WELLBEING IN EARLY YEARS SETTINGS

Strategies and Tools for Practitioners and Teachers

Edited by HELEN SUTHERLAND and YASMIN MUKADAM

Foreword by ANNE RAWLINGS

Jessica Kingsley *Publishers*
London and Philadelphia

First published in 2018
by Jessica Kingsley Publishers
73 Collier Street
London N1 9BE, UK
and
400 Market Street, Suite 400
Philadelphia, PA 19106, USA

www.jkp.com

Copyright © Jessica Kingsley Publishers 2018
Foreword copyright © Anne Rawlings 2018

Front cover image source: iStockphoto®.

Library of Congress Cataloging in Publication Data
Names: Sutherland, Helen, editor. | Mukadam, Yasmin, editor.
Title: Supporting toddlers' wellbeing in early years settings : strategies
    and tools for practitioners and teachers / edited by Helen Sutherland and
    Yasmin Mukadam.
Description: London ; Philadelphia : Jessica Kingsley Publishers, 2018. |
    Includes bibliographical references and index.
Identifiers: LCCN 2017060858 | ISBN 9781785922626 (alk. paper)
Subjects: LCSH: Early childhood education. | Classroom environment. |
    Well-being. | Early childhood development. | Toddlers--Care.
Classification: LCC LB1139.23 .S86 2018 | DDC 372.21--dc23
LC record available at https://lccn.loc.gov/2017060858

British Library Cataloguing in Publication Data
A CIP catalogue record for this book is available from the British Library

ISBN 978 1 78592 262 6
eISBN 978 1 78450 552 3

Printed and bound in the United States

Contents

Foreword

I feel honoured to write the foreword to this book written by two knowledgeable, professional and experienced members of the early years team who I had the pleasure to work with for over 12 years. It is a testament to the authors that they were able to produce a book in the midst of hectic schedules ensuring rigorous research, working with practitioners, children and teachers within a 'transnational' structure. This included work shadowing which enabled practitioners and teachers to share their expertise and reflections on furthering knowledge and understanding of children's wellbeing locally, nationally and internationally throughout the 'ToWe (Toddler Wellbeing) Project' (2015–2018).

Reflection lies at the heart of transformational change and this book will more than meet the needs of a wide range of students and multi professional practitioners working with young children by providing a wealth of opportunities for reflection on theory and practice illuminated in each chapter.

Reflection requires a range of skills and knowledge including how to think about outcomes and then to apply new thinking to complex situations within the workplace environment. This book embeds both purpose and ethics in the approach used to enhance theory and practice of health and wellbeing by posing questions that require reflective thinking on several levels as well as further guidance on reading, research and reviews of how other countries such as Norway and Spain address health and wellbeing provision.

Definitions are given for practitioners to explore links between health, physical and social wellbeing and how these can impact upon mental health. Crucial to all these aspects is the environment within which children live, learn and play. Chapter 4 provides innovative ways of thinking about the environment beyond the physical such as reflecting on the attitude of staff in creating a safe, challenging and motivating learning environment. The reflections by practitioners taking part in this project facilitated the development of a set of helpful indicators such as tone of voice, respect for each other, positive relationships and use of space. The authors provide many opportunities for practitioners to '*challenge their certainties*' through on-going reflections.

Chapter 7 by Cristina Corcoll and Carme Flores, Chapter 8 by Àngels Geis and Chapter 9 by Helen Sutherland and Yasmin Mukadam are interlinked through language development, how to enable the most effective learning environment and consider ways of using different audit tools to action reflections. In Chapter 6 Yngve Rosell and Monika Röthle present different perspectives on adults' and toddlers' views on play demonstrating the importance of being able to listen to the child's voice, to hear what they are saying and to respect their interpretation of play. This will impact on provision and practice depending on the adult's attitude to play and may mean adapting to the child's interest and conditions. Often this can be difficult to resolve depending on a range of issues such as parents' attitudes to play, legal and statutory requirements and theoretical, research and environmental factors.

None of the authors have shied away from confronting thorny issues but have provided a framework of reflective questions for enabling discussion that recognises strengths and areas for development, and to have the confidence to action change.

What this book achieves is support for early years practitioners, teachers, academics, students and multi professional practitioners across a range of countries to reflect deeply and to recognise that by sharing good practice, scholarship and working ethically and collaboratively on contemporary issues, they can envision and action future possibilities for early years education.

Anne Rawlings
Early Years Consultant
Associate Professor Kingston University (Rtd.)
Honorary Early Years Fellow Kingston University

Acknowledgements

I would like to say thank you to our Setting Partners from the ToWe Project, whose dedication, motivation, contribution, energy and enthusiasm has been boundless in their contribution to this book and to the ToWe Project, making this book possible, and for having such a positive impact on toddlers' lives and wellbeing.

Achieving for Children
Alison McGee from Achieving for Children, Janette Barber from Heathfield Children's Centre, Kathryn Hogarth, Tom Maybey and Rachel Lazarides from KMBES (Kew, Mortlake, Barnes and East Sheen) Children's Centres.

Sandvedhaugen Barnehage – Sandnes Kommune
Ingrid Eikeland Andersen, Liv Hjertø, Maj Gabrielsen, Harrieth Elin Kristiansen Strøm, Lillian Bakken, and Nicolle De Graaf from Sandvedhaugen Barnehage and Gudrun Skancke Eriksen from Sandnes Kommune.

Petita Escola
Natàlia Turmo and Sílvia Turmo.

Escola Bressil Mas Balmanya – Suara Serveis
Mireia Miralpeix Anglerill, Maria Jose Riella, Maria Àngels Domènech Pou and Anna Nicolau.

Thank you to my partner authors, Yasmin, Monika, Yngve, Cristina, Carme and Àngels who have been such an amazing team to work with.

Also thank you to Kingston University, School of Education for their support and encouragement and to the British Council and the European Commission for funding the ToWe Project, which has provided the foundations for this book and can be described as the ToWe Project (2015–2018) Enhancing the Education and Wellbeing of Disadvantaged Toddlers through the Development of Training and Materials to Support Early Years Practitioners. ERASMUS+, Key Action 2, School Education Strategic Partnership Project. [2015-1-UK01-013431].

Lastly to Jan Styman, a friend and ex-colleague who has always provided fantastic encouragement and support, thank you.

Preface

Recognition of the importance of wellbeing has come to the fore within early years over the last couple of decades, first with Professor Ferre Laevers *et al.*'s Well Being and Involvement Scales (2005) and then with the United Nations International Children's Emergency Fund (UNICEF) and their Wellbeing Reports. These reports and research have impacted upon UK government legislation and policy with the introduction of Every Child Matters (DfE, 2003) economic wellbeing being introduced into early years and now the *Wellbeing in Four Policy Areas: Report by the All-Party Parliamentary Group on Wellbeing Economics* (All Party Parliamentary Group on Wellbeing Economics, 2014). These have impacted upon early years' provision with the implicit embedding of wellbeing within the early years foundation stage (DfE, 2017). What this means to early years practitioners and teachers (EYPTs) can be different, and how to support this sometimes intangible.

This book hopes to address this by exploring the context and definitions of wellbeing within Chapter 1, drawing upon both national and international perspectives. Chapter 1 will also introduce the reader to the importance of reflective practice and using reflective practice to support wellbeing within their setting.

With the introduction of free early education and childcare for two-year-olds (FEET) funding for toddlers within the UK, more early years settings are in receipt of vulnerable and disadvantaged toddlers (DfE, 2014). How these toddlers are valued – and their learning and development supported – is vital in helping them to reach their full potential.

To help achieve this, the Toddler Wellbeing (ToWe) Project was developed to improve the practice of EYPTs so that they, in turn, would be better able to support toddlers' wellbeing (ToWe Project, 2015–2018). To accomplish this, project materials, tools and audits were developed and training provided to the EYPTs from the setting partners within the project, who in turn have used these materials, tools and audits to inform and improve their provision and practice. They have worked with their colleagues within their settings to support their knowledge and understanding of supporting toddler wellbeing, implementing a variety of strategies to improve the opportunities for their toddlers.

A holistic approach was used in developing the materials, with reflection being at the heart of this. Opportunities to share practice, expertise and learning from each other were provided through job shadowing, where the EYPTs from the setting partners participated in transnational mobility. They were able to observe and work together, visiting each others' countries and settings. This enabled them to reflect upon the similarities and differences between each country (England, Norway and Spain) and how they were all working to support toddlers' wellbeing. They were able to discuss and reflect upon the various strategies that they had developed to support toddler wellbeing.

The work of the ToWe Project has informed and provided the foundation for this book, and reference is made to the project and materials. The book develops the subject of how to support toddlers' wellbeing further, building upon the materials from the project. This can be seen within the dimensions which provide the headings for each chapter. These chapters are intended to support the reader in reflecting upon their setting's provision and practice, identifying where they could possibly develop and improve upon what they are currently doing. The chapters can be used separately or together as the content of the book has been designed to be adaptable and flexible in its usage as the tools and strategies compliment and support each other in encouraging reflection on how to enhance and improve opportunities for toddler wellbeing.

Within each chapter of the book there are questions to support the reader's reflections of their own provision and practice. The EYPTs from the ToWe Project partner settings provide reflections from their experiences and strategies that they have developed to support toddlers' wellbeing.

Each chapter within the book covers a dimension of wellbeing, informed from a range of different sources that address wellbeing: for example, UNICEF Wellbeing Report cards (UNICEF, 2013). Using this information, the ToWe Project came up with the 'Toddlers' Wellbeing Framework' that identified the dimensions of wellbeing. We have continued to use these dimensions within the book using them to write the following chapters:

Family, Home and Environmental Factors (Chapter 2)

Health of Toddlers (Chapter 3)

Setting Environments (Chapter 4)

Development and Learning (Chapter 5)

Expressions in Play (Chapter 6)

Early Languages (Chapter 7)

Mealtimes (Chapter 8)

The chapters explore the chosen dimensions of wellbeing, with Chapter 2 investigating the concepts of parent partnership, the impact of home environment and the effects that environmental factors such as housing and providing a safe and stimulating environment within the home have upon toddlers' wellbeing.

Chapter 3 looks at how physical and mental health, childhood illnesses, toddlers' individual needs and abilities and other factors may inhibit their wellbeing. This chapter also explores how EYPTs can promote health and wellbeing with toddlers.

Chapter 4 explores how the setting environment can provide play and learning opportunities for toddlers, with consideration of Health and Safety while enabling risk taking. It also addresses aspects of staffing, practitioner training, experience and qualifications, as well as the staff's role in being a professional and the key person approach in supporting toddlers' wellbeing.

Chapter 5 considers how toddlers develop and learn to reach their full potential, looking at personal, social, emotional and spiritual interaction, engagement and play, attachment and settling-in. It makes links to Chapter 8 in relation to meal and snack times, and also links to Chapters 6 and 7 regarding toddlers' voices, expressions and early languages. This chapter also includes cognitive, language and comm-unication, physical abilities and attitudes and behaviour relating to emotional resilience, regulating feelings and behaviours.

Chapter 6 explores the political and theoretical background and literature in supporting toddlers' voices and expressions. It describes the UN Convention on the Rights of the Child (UNCRC), changes and research on the views of toddlers, and the EYPT's role in supporting toddlers' voices and expressions in play.

Chapter 7 explores how early childhood education should provide toddlers with the best learning opportunities, focusing on language and language learning, including adapting the plurilingual approach to the toddlers' needs and abilities. It addresses different linguistic realities and culture, welcoming identities within the setting, and bringing new languages and cultures into the setting. It explores how Outdoor Content and Language Integrated Learning at School/Settings (O'CLILS) can be used to support toddlers early languages.

Chapter 8 explores mealtimes and how toddlers' routines, educational spaces, mealtimes culture and the meal quality have an impact upon toddlers' wellbeing.

Chapter 9 concludes the book by identifying the impact and value of the tools and strategies provided to support toddler wellbeing throughout this book and the ToWe Project. It highlights the research and some of the results and impact of the project. The chapter also considers how you can develop your future vision for enhancing the quality and opportunities for toddler wellbeing, engaging staff to fully embrace and successfully implement toddler wellbeing within your setting.

I hope that this book provides you, the reader, with the help, support, ideas and strategies to engage in improving and developing the opportunities for the toddlers within your setting, so that they might have a strong and healthy wellbeing.

Helen Sutherland

References

DfE (2003) *Every Child Matters.* Accessed 29 January 2018 at https://www.gov.uk/government/uploads/system/uploads/attachment_data/file/272064/5860.pdf

DfE (2014) *Early Years Pupil Premium and funding for two-year-olds.* Accessed 29 January 2018 at https://www.gov.uk/government/uploads/system/uploads/attachment_data/file/323495/EY_Funding_ConDoc_-Branded_final_with_foreword.pdf

DfE (2017) *Statutory Framework for the Early Years Foundation Stage: Setting the Standards for Learning, Development and Care for Children from Birth to Five.* Accessed 29 January 2018 at https://www.foundationyears.org.uk/files/2017/03/EYFS_STATUTORY_FRAMEWORK_2017.pdf

Laevers, F., Daems, M., De Bruyckere, G., Declercq, B. *et al.* (2005) SICS. *Well-being and Involvement in Care. A Process-oriented Self-evaluation Instrument for Care Settings.* Accessed 29 January 2018 at https://www.kindengezin.be/img/sics-ziko-manual.pdf

ToWe Project (2015–2018) *Enhancing the Education and Wellbeing of Disadvantaged Toddlers through the Development of Training and Materials to Support Early Years Practitioners.* ERASMUS+, Key Action 2, School Education Strategic Partnership Project. [2015-1-UK01-013431] Accessed 2 November 2017 at www.toddlerswellbeing.eu

UNICEF (2013) *Report Card 11: Child Well-Being in Rich Countries.* Accessed 29 January 2018 at https://www.unicef-irc.org/publications/pdf/rc11_eng.pdf

CHAPTER 1

INTRODUCTION TO THE CONTEXT OF WELLBEING

Helen Sutherland and Yasmin Mukadam

'The true measure of a nation's standing is how well it attends to its children – their health and safety, their material security, their education and socialization, and their sense of being loved, valued, and included in the families and societies into which they are born.'

————————————— *(UNICEF, 2007)* —————————————

Introduction

This chapter will explore the context, definitions and aspects of wellbeing in early years settings in relation to political and international perspectives. For this, links will be made to the UK government agenda, Organisation for Economic Co-operation and Development (OECD), United Nations International Children's Emergency Fund (UNICEF), definitions of wellbeing, relevant literature, strategies and tools currently in use to support wellbeing.

The term 'wellbeing' has been universally recognised and is common terminology in many early childhood education and care (ECEC) settings. However, there are many differing perspectives and definitions relating to the concept of wellbeing and it is important that early years practitioners and teachers (EYPTs) have a clear understanding of what wellbeing actually is in relation to their own perspectives and practice.

The international context of wellbeing

The United Nations Convention on the Rights of the Child (UNCRC) recognised 'that the child, for the full and harmonious development of his or her personality, should grow up in a family environment, in an atmosphere of happiness, love and understanding' (UNICEF, 1989). This encapsulates all that wellbeing entails, and the requirements of meeting these needs today and for the future, both in relation to the rights of the toddler and their learning and development.

Since 2000, UNICEF has been making comparisons on child poverty within rich nations, leading to international league tables on child poverty presented in Innocenti Report Cards, providing 'comprehensive estimates so far of child poverty across the industrialized world' (UNICEF, 2000). This has led to ongoing reports on child wellbeing; in particular, UNICEF's Report Card 11: Child Well-Being in Rich Countries (UNICEF, 2013). The scores from this report highlighted that wellbeing in the United Kingdom was ranked at 16th out of 29 OECD members of developed countries co-operating in this report. Norway was ranked 2nd with Spain being ranked 19th.

Another key document was from Education, Audiovisual and Culture Executive Agency (EACEA, 2009) 'Early Childhood Education and Care in Europe: Tackling Social and Cultural Inequalities', which highlighted the importance of how effective pre-school education can promote life-long learning and provide opportunities to increase equality by supporting children in reaching their full potential. This is especially important in supporting diverse and disadvantaged children and their families. Your role and attitude, as EYPTs, is therefore vital in creating 'a positive socio-emotional climate, with emotionally safe and stable relationships, with sensitive-responsive, non-intrusive teachers' (EACEA, 2009).

The national context for England, Norway and Spain
England

The UK government provided a national context for England by identifying its commitment to halving child poverty by 2010 and eradicating it by 2020. The introduction of the Every Child Matters (ECM) (DfE, 2003) agenda was a key strategy for supporting wellbeing in childhood and later life, based upon five outcomes:

1. Be healthy.

2. Stay safe.

3. Enjoy and achieve.

4. Make a positive contribution.

5. Achieve economic wellbeing.

This agenda underpinned the Children Act 2004, and the Childcare Act 2006, which created a basis for the early years foundation stage (EYFS) framework. This has led to a number of pivotal pieces of research, government reporting and developments:

- The Effective Provision of Pre-School Education Project (Sylva *et al.*, 2004) was the first longitudinal study of its kind in England, exploring different provisions and how good practice influenced a child's development.

- The Key Elements of Effective Practice carried out for the Department for Education and Skills (DfES) now the Department for Education (DfE) emphasised that 'effective learning is dependent on secure relationships, and appropriate learning environment and high-quality teaching' (DfES, 2005).

- The Allen Report (2011) highlighted children's social and emotional development as a 'bedrock' in supporting children's physical and mental health. Allen identified that early intervention was imperative for the foundations of children's social and emotional development 'which will help to keep them happy, healthy and achieving throughout their lives and, above all, equip them to raise children of their own, who will also enjoy higher levels of wellbeing' (Allen, 2011).

- The Tickell Report (2011) provided a comprehensive review of the EYFS, drawing on the Allen Report (2011), and reviewed four areas:

  1. regulation

  2. learning and development

  3. assessment

  4. welfare.

- The EYFS continued to ensure that children's wellbeing is promoted through a variety of strategies put forward by Allen (2011) and Tickell (2011), including the Two Year Progress Check carried out by EYPTs on all children that attend early years settings (DfE, 2012).

- The EYFS framework (DfE, 2014b) was revised however continued to include aspects of wellbeing and the key person approach, but in less detail than previously.

- Through early education entitlement, early years pupil premium (EYPP) and free early education and childcare for two-year-olds (FEET), currently all three- to four-year-olds in England are entitled to 570 hours of free early education or childcare per year. The EYPP provides support for additional funding for early years settings to improve the education they provide for disadvantaged three- and four-year-olds. Alongside this, FEET is also now available from the child's second birthday for toddlers and their families who meet the criteria (DfE, 2014a, 2015).

- In September 2014 the government published an all parties policy objective on wellbeing identifying four key areas for development, one of which is 'Building personal resources: mindfulness in health and Education' (All Party Parliamentary Group on Wellbeing Economics, 2014).

- Following on from the above report, recommendations were published within the Mindful Nation UK Report (All Party Parliamentary Group on Wellbeing Economics, 2015) which introduced mindfulness as an approach to reduce the mental health crisis which is increasing in the UK. This sought to introduce mindfulness interventions within the areas of education and health. The report identifies an emerging body of evidence that suggests both parents and children can benefit from the practice of mindfulness (Sutherland and Mukadam, 2018).

Norway

The UN for several years has ranked Norway as the best country in the world to live in, stated in the Human Development Index (United Nations Development Programme, 2015). There is also however a growing proportion of children in Norway who are living in poverty. In Norway the following legislation is in place to support children's wellbeing:

- The 2005 Kindergarten Act update was enforced in 2010 under decree number 828. This act highlights the importance of wellbeing within early childhood, stating that kindergartens should: trust and respect children, understanding that this is an essential part of childhood; provide 'wellbeing and joy in play and learning, and shall be a challenging and safe place for community life and friendship' by countering discrimination of all forms and promoting equality and democracy (Kindergarten Act, 2005, 2010).

- The Framework Plan for the Content and Tasks of Kindergartens (Ministry of Education and Research, 2011) explains further how Norway takes responsibility for children's wellbeing and development linking to the Kindergarten Acts 2005, 2010 which identify that play is natural and that children should have chances for self-expression in their play. It is important that kindergartens contribute to supporting children's childhood and all round development and learning, offering opportunities for play, which 'is of importance for the wellbeing of the children and as a fundamental aspect of life and learning'.

- The very first Framework Plan was introduced in 1995 and builds on the Norwegian Kindergarten tradition with this being updated in 2006 and 2011. The Framework Plan emphasises the role of the kindergarten in engaging children's experience, exploration and learning (Sutherland and Mukadam, 2018).

Spain

The term 'wellbeing' is not directly referred to within government documentation but the concept of wellbeing is implicit within the main early childhood education goals. *Ley Orgánica para la Mejora de la Calidad Educativa* (LOMCE) translates as Organic Law for the Improvement of Educational Quality (Ministry of Education, Culture and Sport, 2013), publicly announced in the Agencia Estatal Boletín Oficial del Estado which sets the curriculum framework for each municipality to expand upon. It highlights that 'Education shall be directed to the full development of human personality in respect for the democratic principles of coexistence and the rights and fundamental freedoms' (Ministry of Education, Culture and Sport, 2013). It highlights that the educational system should differentiate teaching and learning to meet students' needs as they have been changing with society.

> Education is the key to this transformation through the formation of people [who are] active with self-confidence, curious, enterprising and innovative, eager to participate in the society to which they belong, to create individual and collective value, capable of assuming as their own the value of the balance between effort and reward. (Ministry of Education, Culture and Sport, 2013)

In early childhood education in Catalan Spain the concept of wellbeing is recognised within the main goals of the curriculum where it contributes to all aspects of child development and learning, providing a welcoming environment conducive to learning (Departament D'Educació, 2010). The document also goes on to say that the educational action 'must allow emotional development, personal growth of children and formation of a balanced and positive image of themselves' (Department D'Educació, 2010).

⟳ REFLECTION 1.1

Reflect upon the impact that your government legislation and initiatives have had on your setting's provision and practice.

Definitions of wellbeing

As mentioned in the introduction, the term 'wellbeing' is widely used within ECEC settings. It is important to have a clear understanding at the outset of your own perspectives, values and beliefs regarding this terminology as this varies between EYPTs and different countries.

In Belgium, Ferre Laevers has been working with the subject of wellbeing since the 1970s, setting up the educational model of Experiential Education (EXE) in assessing the quality of educational provision in ECEC settings. He defines what wellbeing is and what it entails identifying that it is important to know how each child is getting on within the setting by observing how self-confident and comfortable they are accessing the provision of the setting. This provides a baseline to their emotional wellbeing, that it is fine 'and that their physical needs, the need for tenderness and affection, the need for safety and clarity, the need for social recognition, the need to feel competent and the need for meaning and moral value in life are satisfied' (Laevers, 2005). Interventions can then be developed to support and strengthen children's wellbeing, helping them to understand their emotions and feeling.

Statham and Chase (2010) define the term wellbeing as 'a dynamic state that is enhanced when people can fulfil their personal and social goals'. They emphasise that childhood wellbeing is:

> not only complex but multi-dimensional, and should include dimensions of physical, social and emotional well-being; it should focus on the immediate lives of children but also consider their future lives; and should incorporate some subjective as well as objective measures.

⟳ REFLECTION 1.2

Identify what the definition of wellbeing means to you and how this is reflected within your daily provision and practice.

Here are three definitions of wellbeing from the Towards Opportunities for Disadvantaged and Diverse Learners on the Early childhood Road (TODDLER) Project (2013):

England

> Wellbeing is a state of being or condition of existence that characterises an individual realising their full potential through their own prosperity, welfare, life satisfaction, health, eudemonia (human flourishing) and happiness.

Norway

Wellbeing is a positive physical, mental and social state. It is enhanced by conditions that include positive personal relationships with adults and peers, an environment that promotes challenging indoor and outdoor play activities, and an inclusive community that allows the individual child to experience joy and happiness, to unfold his/her potential and to express his/her view on the ongoing activities.

Spain

Creating the necessary conditions so that children's wellbeing can be guaranteed is the axis around which the main aims of Infant Education 0–3 (early childhood education) revolve. Wellbeing is the physical and emotional state that lets the child fully develop his/her autonomy according to his/her possibilities, individually or in relation with others, in a specific context and through different languages, considering each and every need they have, every instinct and ability.

The Toddlers' Wellbeing Framework

The Toddlers' Wellbeing Framework provides a theoretical framework that represents the complexity and relationship between learning, development and societal systems that can be applied in supporting toddlers' wellbeing. This framework identifies the different dimensions relating to wellbeing with four pedagogical characteristics to support understanding and application of these dimensions for EYPTs (see Figure 1.1).

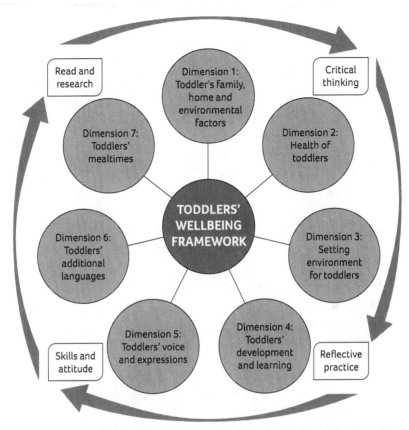

Figure 1.1 – Toddlers' Wellbeing Framework (Sutherland and Mukadam, 2018)

Using the four pedagogical characteristics

These four pedagogical characteristics underpin the essential traits in developing the knowledge and understanding practitioners and teachers require in supporting toddlers' progress and outcomes. This framework represents the various elements of a toddler's life coming together. The four characteristics are as follows:

1. Read and research

2. Critical thinking

3. Reflective practice

4. Skills and attitudes

(ToWe Project, 2015–2018)

1. Read and research

Keeping up to date and engaging with current thinking and research is vital to enhancing knowledge and understanding of trends within early years and the impact that these might have upon provision and processes within settings. Selecting the most relevant sources is an important starting point to reading the appropriate literature that will inform and challenge your provision and practice. Accessing the right types of websites is crucial so that you are accessing reliable and accurate sites, such as Foundation Years, which provides up-to-date government legislation and initiatives.

The reading skills required to be able to achieve this are the ability to 'scan and skim read' and identify the key points. Prior to reading any literature, identify what the key words are to support the area of reading within your chosen literature. To check the relevance and reliability of a source, you should identify:

- the author. This may be a government organisation, university, local authority, voluntary organisation or a reputable business organisation. This may be for the whole site or particular page.

- the date it was last updated and published. If archived, is this still relevant or is there a more up-to-date source available?

- the country of origin. How does this apply to your home country's ECEC provision and practice?

♻ REFLECTION 1.3

Research the topic of 'wellbeing' using the internet:

» Identify three reliable sites.

» Use the key words:

     – Emotional wellbeing

     – Resilience

     – Self-confidence

» Scan and skim read the chosen document.

» Summarise your findings.

2. Critical thinking

Critical thinking is the ability to think critically, evaluating and reflecting upon any given situation to make informed judgements upon provision and practice with consideration of the wider context. This is an active process involving engagement and application of knowledge, analysis of concepts and synthesis of understanding to achieve and develop new understanding, values and beliefs which can be applied through this learning process. It is through this process that critical thinking skills are evolved promoting creativity of thought and reflection and it is necessary for the revision and development of provision in meeting toddlers' needs. It is through being open and willing to engage in critical thinking that practice can be developed as we open ourselves up to new possibilities. This however is not always an easy thing to do as it may challenge our current beliefs and values.

♻ REFLECTION 1.4

Using the 'Toddlers' Wellbeing Framework' identify the dimension that is most prominent within your setting.

> » Consider how the wider context has influenced your setting's provision.

> » Critically analyse what impact this has had on your practice and why.

> » What new understanding have you gained and how can this be applied within your practice?

3. Reflective practice

Reflection is a process of thoughtful consideration of any given situation. EYPTs can use reflection to unpack and explore the issues arising from both their personal and professional practice. This thoughtful consideration starts the process of actively engaging in continuous self-appraised thought in order to understand what is happening, why this maybe happening, what is the wider context underpinning this and how this could be addressed.

This is important in order to improve, challenge and raise the levels of provision and practice within settings. Using reflective models can be helpful in developing further depth to the criticality of the reflective process you engage in. This includes the process of:

- describing what has happened

- interpreting what this means

- analysing to make sense of this by drawing upon the wider context of the situation

- creating a plan of action.

⟳ REFLECTION 1.5

Look up one of the following models:

» Describe, Feelings, Evaluation, Analysis, Conclusion and Action Plan (Gibbs, 1988)

» Descriptive, Perceptive, Receptive, Interactive and Critical (Ghaye and Ghaye, 1998)

» What? So what? What now? (Rolfe, Freshwater and Jasper, 2001)

Using a chosen model, reflect upon what you have learnt from the source relating to wellbeing from the previous reflective task.

4. Skills and attitudes

Positive skills and attitudes are key characteristics for developing secure and trusting relationships with toddlers. A sound knowledge and understanding of toddlers' wellbeing is imperative when supporting their development and learning as this enables effective engagement and awareness of toddlers' individual needs. Three key components to developing and supporting toddlers' wellbeing are highlighted in Figure 1.2.

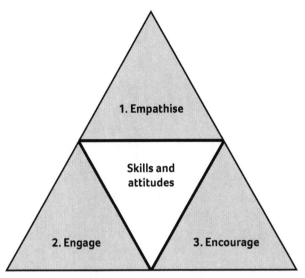

Figure 1.2 – Key components to developing and supporting toddlers' wellbeing (Sutherland and Mukadam, 2018)

These key components are vital in managing situations effectively as having empathy supports relationship building as links and understanding are demonstrated; while engaging helps to develop strategies to improve the situation while encouraging others to be involved.

⟳ REFLECTION 1.6

Identify three further key components that support the characteristic of skills and attitudes.

How can these key components be further demonstrated to enhance your provision and practice?

Dimensions and aspects of wellbeing

As identified at the start of the chapter, UNICEF have been comparing and reporting on child poverty within rich nations (UNICEF, 2000). The key findings highlighted that the United Kingdom was ranked within the bottom four for 'relative child poverty'. Spain was ranked within the bottom four for 'absolute child poverty'; while in contrast Norway was ranked in the top two countries for both 'relative and absolute poverty'.

Relative Poverty	Absolute Poverty
'Families lack the income required and live below the average standard of living for the country and society that they live in. They are considered impoverished if they cannot maintain the living standards of society.'	'Families lack the minimum income required to meet one or more of basic minimum needs for living and sustaining life.'

(Sutherland and Mukadam, 2018)

Report Card 6 (UNICEF, 2005) measured child poverty in 24 OECD countries highlighting that poverty had increased in seventeen of these countries. This led to Report Card 7 (UNICEF, 2007) measuring child wellbeing in 21 OECD countries. Six dimensions were used with separate indicators to measure key aspects of child wellbeing rather than using income poverty as a measure. This was to support OECD countries in prioritising change and improvement through government initiatives and strategies. The six dimensions were:

1. Material wellbeing

2. Health and safety

3. Education

4. Peer and family relationships

5. Behaviours and risks

6. Young people's own subjective sense of wellbeing.

(UNICEF, 2007)

Report Card 11 (UNICEF, 2013) measured child wellbeing within 29 OECD countries using five dimensions with separate indicators. This report card updated and enhanced the key findings from Report Card 7 while summarising and identifying trends linking to child wellbeing in rich countries. The five dimensions were:

1. Material Well-being

2. Health

3. Education

4. Behaviour and Risk

5. Housing and Environment.

(UNICEF, 2013)

Leuven wellbeing and involvement scales

Professor Ferre Laevers and his team at the Research Centre for Experiential Education at Leuven University, Belgium, designed a set of wellbeing involvement scales, Leuven Involvement Scales (LIS), so that EYPTs could develop and improve the quality of their provision using these self-assessment tools. These scales are part of the model for experiential education that enables EYPTs to focus on key children and score their wellbeing and involvement as part of the process-oriented approach (Laevers, 2015). Within the scale, the two dimensions of this model support not just emotional wellbeing but recognise the importance of involvement. The dimension of involvement relates to the level of activity and engagement that the child experiences within their setting, this is important for 'deep level learning and development' (Laevers *et al.*, 2005), whereas the dimension of wellbeing refers to how the child is feeling so that they can express their feelings in a healthy and positive way.

Observation is an important tool within this process as it is used to assess the wellbeing and involvement of children. The three steps used within the process-oriented approach are:

- Step 1: Assessment of wellbeing and involvement

- Step 2: Analysis of observation

- Step 3: Improving what you can and what next?

(Laevers *et al.*, 2005)

Sustained Shared Thinking and Emotional Wellbeing Scales (SSTEW)

This environmental rating scale is important in measuring social, emotional and cognitive development of children from two to five years. These three domains are key in creating the Developmentally Appropriate Practice (DAP). This supports quality, improvement and development of practice within settings. The adult's role in this is to support children's learning and development using the pedagogical strategies to support their practice, within the domains of sustained shared thinking and emotional wellbeing.

The longitudinal research studies of The Effective Provision of Pre-school Education (EPPE) (Sylva *et al.*, 2004) and Researching

Effective Pedagogy in the Early Years (REPEY) (Siraj-Blatchford *et al.*, 2002) influenced the development of SSTEW and promoted the value of EYPTs' active engagement in supporting toddlers' learning (ToWe Project, 2015–2018).

The SSTEW rating scales are completed through observations of children within all areas of the setting by EYPTs. They use their professional judgement in ranking, from one to seven, the setting's practice under the following headings:

Sub-scale 1: building trust, confidence and independence

Sub-scale 2: social and emotional well-being

Sub-scale 3: supporting and extending language and communication

Sub-scale 4: supporting learning and critical thinking

Sub-scale 5: assessing learning and language.

(Siraj, Kingston and Melhuish, 2015)

⟳ REFLECTION 1.7

Look at the UNICEF Report Cards, Leuven Involvement Scales and Sustained Shared Thinking and Emotional Wellbeing (SSTEW) Scales.

Investigate one of these further and consider how this impacts or could impact upon your setting's quality of provision and practice.

Conclusion

This chapter has explored the international and national contexts of wellbeing, defining what this means and the emerging perspectives underpinning government agendas in England, Norway and Spain. The 'Toddlers' Wellbeing Framework' introduced the seven dimensions.

These dimensions identify aspects that support toddlers' general wellbeing similar to the UNICEF dimensions. This holistic approach interweaves and impacts upon each dimension and will be used to examine and support the development of toddlers' wellbeing while applying the four pedagogical characteristics. The following seven chapters will explore each of these dimensions providing strategies and tools for supporting toddlers' wellbeing.

References

All Party Parliamentary Group on Wellbeing Economics (2014) *Wellbeing in four policy areas.* Accessed 21 November 2017 at http://b.3cdn.net/nefoundation/ccdf9782b6d8700f7c_lcm6i2ed7.pdf

All Party Parliamentary Group on Wellbeing Economics (2015) *Mindful Nation UK Report by the Mindfulness All-Party Parliamentary Group (MAPPG).* Accessed 21 November 2017 at http://www.themindfulnessinitiative.org.uk/images/reports/Mindfulness-APPG-Report_Mindful-Nation-UK_Oct2015.pdf

Allen, G. (2011) *Early intervention: The next steps.* Accessed 21 November 2017 at https://www.gov.uk/government/publications/early-intervention-the-next-steps--2

Childcare Act 2006, c. 21. Accessed 21 November 2017 at www.legislation.gov.uk/ukpga/2006/21/contents

Children Act 2004, c. 31. Accessed 21 November 2017 at www.legislation.gov.uk/ukpga/2004/31/contents

Departament D'Educació (2010) *Diari Oicial de la Generalitat de Catalunya Núm 5686.* Accessed 5 December 2017 at http://portaldogc.gencat.cat/utilsEADOP/PDF/5686/1104618.pdf

DfE (2003) *Every Child Matters.* Accessed 21 November 2017 at https://www.gov.uk/government/uploads/system/uploads/attachment_data/file/272064/5860.pdf

DfE (2012) *Statutory Framework for the Early Years Foundation Stage: Setting the standards for learning, development and care for children from birth to five.* Accessed 21 November 2017 at http://webarchive.nationalarchives.gov.uk/20130401151715/https://www.education.gov.uk/publications/eOrderingDownload/EYFS%20Statutory%20Framework.pdf

DfE (2014a) *Early Years Pupil Premium and funding for two-year-olds.* Accessed 21 November 2017 at https://www.gov.uk/government/uploads/system/uploads/attachment_data/file/323495/EY_Funding_ConDoc_-Branded_final_with_foreword.pdf

DfE (2014b) *Statutory Framework for the Early Years Foundation Stage: Setting the standards for learning, development and care for children from birth to five.* Accessed 21 November 2017 at https://www.gov.uk/government/uploads/system/uploads/attachment_data/file/335504/EYFS_framework_from_1_September_2014__with_clarification_note.pdf

DfE (2015) *Free childcare and education for 3- and 4-year-olds.* Accessed 21 November 2017 at https://www.gov.uk/help-with-childcare-costs/free-childcare-and-education-for-2-to-4-year-olds

DfES (2005) *KEEP – Key Elements of Effective Practice.* Accessed 21 November 2017 at http://dera.ioe.ac.uk/7593/7/pns_fs120105keep_Redacted.pdf

EACEA (2009) *Early Childhood Education and Care in Europe: Tackling Social and Cultural Inequalities.* European Commission. Accessed 2 November 2017 at http://eacea.ec.europa.eu/about/eurydice/documents/098EN.pdf

Ghaye, T. and Ghaye, K. (1998) *Teaching and Learning Through Critical Reflective Practice.* London: David Fulton.

Gibbs, G. (1988) *Learning by Doing: A Guide to Teaching and Learning Methods.* Oxford: Oxford Polytechnic.

Kindergarten Act (2005, 2010) Act number 64. Accessed 21 November 2017 at https://www.regjeringen.no/en/dokumenter/kindergarten-act/id115281/

Laevers, F. (2005) *Experiential Education – Deep Level Learning in Early Childhood and Primary Education.* University of Leuven. Accessed 2 November 2017 at https://vorming.cego.be/images/downloads/BO_DP_Deep-levelLearning.pdf (6)

Laevers, F., Daems, M., De Bruyckere G., Declercq B. *et al.* (2005) SICS. *Well-being and Involvement in Care. A Process-oriented Self-evaluation Instrument for Care Settings.* Accessed 22 December 2017 at https://www.kindengezin.be/img/sics-ziko-manual.pdf

Laevers, F. (2015) *Making care and education more effective through wellbeing and involvement. An introduction to Experiential Education.* Accessed 22 December 2017 at https://vorming.cego.be/images/downloads/Ond_DP_IntroductionExpEduc.pdf

Ministry of Education, Culture and Sport. (2013) *Ley Orgánica 8/2013, de 9 de diciembre, para la mejora de la calidad educative.* Accessed 21 November 2017 at www.boe.es/diario_boe/txt.php?id=BOE-A-2013-12886

Ministry of Education and Research (2006) *Framework Plan for the Content and Tasks of Kindergartens.* Accessed 21 November 2017 at https://www.regjeringen.no/globalassets/upload/KD/Vedlegg/Barnehager/engelsk/FrameworkPlanfortheContentandTasksofKindergartens.pdf

Ministry of Education and Research (2011) *Framework Plan for the Content and Tasks of Kindergartens.* Accessed 21 November 2017 at www.udir.no/Upload/barnehage/Rammeplan/Framework_Plan_for_the_Content_and_Tasks_of_Kindergartens_2011_rammeplan_engelsk.pdf

Rolfe, G., Freshwater, D. and Jasper, M. (2001) *Critical Reflection in Nursing and the Helping Professions: A User's Guide.* Basingstoke: Palgrave Macmillan.

Siraj I., Kingston, D. and Melhuish, E. (2015) *Assessing Quality in Early Childhood Education and Care: Sustained Shared Thinking and Emotional Wellbeing (SSTEW) Scale for 2–5-year-olds Provision.* London: IOE Press.

Siraj-Blatchford, I., Sylva, K., Muttock, S., Gilden, R. and Bell, D. (2002) *Researching Effective Pedagogy in the Early Years (REPEY).* London: DfES.

Statham, J. and Chase, E. (2010) *Childhood Well-being: A Brief Overview.* Loughborough: Childhood Wellbeing Research Centre. Accessed 2 November 2017 at https://www.education.gov.uk/publications/eOrderingDownload/Child-Wellbeing-Brief.pdf

Sutherland, H. and Mukadam, Y. (2018) *Toddlers' Wellbeing Manual.* ToWe Project 2015–2018. Accessed March 2018 at www.toddlerswellbeing.eu

Sylva, K., Melhuish, E., Sammons, P., Siraj-Blatchford, I. and Taggart, B. (2004) *The Effective Provision of Pre-School Education (EPPE) Project.* Accessed 21 November 2017 at http://webarchive.nationalarchives.gov.uk/20130401151715/https://www.education.gov.uk/publications/eOrderingDownload/SSU-FR-2004-01.pdf

Tickell, C. (2011) *The Early Years: Foundations for life, health and learning.* Accessed 21 November 2017 at https://www.gov.uk/government/uploads/system/uploads/attachment_data/file/180919/DFE-00177-2011.pdf

TODDLER Project (2013) *Towards Opportunities for Disadvantaged and Diverse Learners on the Early-childhood Road.* European Union, Lifelong Learning Programme, Comenius, [61609-LLP-I-2010-NO-COMENIUS-CMP]. Accessed 2 November 2017 at www.toddlerineurope.eu

ToWe Project (2015–2018) *Enhancing the Education and Wellbeing of Disadvantaged Toddlers through the Development of Training and Materials to Support Early Years Practitioners.* ERASMUS+, Key Action 2, School Education Strategic Partnership Project. [2015-1-UK01-013431] Accessed 2 November 2017 at www.toddlerswellbeing.eu

UNICEF (2000) *A League Table of Child Poverty in Rich Nations.* Accessed 2 November 2017 at www.unicef-irc.org/publications/pdf/repcard1e.pdf

UNICEF (2005) *Report Card 6: Child poverty in rich countries: The proportion of children living in poverty has risen in a majority of the world's developed economies.* Accessed 13 February 2018 at www.unicef-irc.org/publications/pdf/repcard6e.pdf

UNICEF (2007) *Report Card 7: Child poverty in perspective: An overview of child well-being in rich countries.* Accessed 2 November 2017 at www.unicef.org/media/files/ChildPovertyReport.pdf

UNICEF (2013) *Report Card 11: Child Well-Being in Rich Countries.* Accessed 2 November 2017 at https://www.unicef-irc.org/publications/683/

UNICEF (1989) *A summary of the UN Convention on the Rights of the Child.* Accessed 13 February 2018 at https://www.unicef.org.uk/wp-content/uploads/2010/05/UNCRC_summary-1.pdf

United Nations Development Programme (2015) *Human Development Index and its components.* Accessed 21 November 2017 at http://hdr.undp.org/en/composite/HDI

CHAPTER 2

FAMILY, HOME AND ENVIRONMENTAL FACTORS

Helen Sutherland and Yasmin Mukadam

'Every child has the right to a standard of living that is good enough to meet their physical, social and mental needs. Governments must help families who cannot afford to provide this.'

(UNICEF UK, 1989)

Introduction

This chapter will investigate the first dimension of the Toddlers' Wellbeing Framework, exploring how early years practitioners and teachers (EYPTs) can work in partnership with parents, carers and families to understand the issues that families may be facing within the home environment. This will include key factors that impact toddlers' wellbeing within the home, such as the socio-economic context, and environmental factors relating to housing and providing a safe and stimulating environment.

EYPTs will be able to gain an insight into the importance of demographics and parents' lifestyle choices upon toddlers and their families. Consideration of linguistic identities and family values will be reflected upon with reflective experiences and strategies provided from England, Norway and Spain. These areas are vital as they impact upon toddlers' development and wellbeing and will also be explored further in future chapters.

Developing partnership with parents, carers and families

As an EYPT it is important to develop positive and trusting partnerships with parents from the outset. The term 'parent' will be used when referring to supporting toddlers' wellbeing as parents are the main caregivers who have the legal responsibilities for making the overall decisions regarding the welfare of their toddler (Children Act, 1989). 'Parents' is being used as a generic term to include guardians and those who have legal responsibility.

Building positive relationships with parents will enable and support effective communication and trust. It is important to be aware that there is a wide range of diverse individuals who have parental responsibilities and will respond to their role in many different ways. Therefore it is the role of EYPTs to understand the differing needs, values, attitudes, beliefs and parenting styles of each, and how this impacts upon your own beliefs, values and attitudes.

When addressing home and environmental factors, it is essential that tact, respect, sensitivity and consideration are given to parents when seeking information or discussing any concerns. This is where parental partnership plays a vital role in establishing a positive relationship in order to support and address the needs of the toddler and family.

⟳ REFLECTION 2.1

Reflect upon how your setting currently develops parental partnerships:

» What strategies do you use that are effective in partnership working?

» How do you maintain professional integrity when working and developing positive and trusting relationships with all parents?

» How do your own beliefs, values and attitudes impact upon your relationships and partnerships with parents?

There are a range of strategies and valuable resources that can be implemented within the setting; these are identified in Figure 2.1.

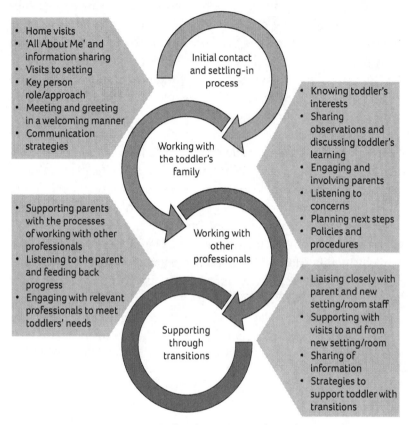

Figure 2.1 – Stages of working in partnership with parents

These stages can help build continuity for the toddler and enhance partnership working between the home and setting. The importance of positive relationships is highlighted in various UK policy documents, including the Early Years Foundation Stage (EYFS) (DfE, 2014, 2017) and Healthy Child Programme (DoH, 2009 and Public Health England, 2015).

It is important to be aware of and keep parents informed of the different funding opportunities that they can access, such as free early education and childcare for two-year-olds (FEET) funding. The Parents, Early Years and Learning (PEAL) Project by the National Children's Bureau (NCB) was commissioned by the DfES over a two-year period to develop a framework of working in partnership with parents, and to develop engagement in their children's learning (Wheeler and Connor, 2006).

It is essential for EYPTs to be aware of their professional boundaries when working collaboratively in partnership parents and other services. It is through having a depth of knowledge about toddlers' development and learning and sharing information in a tactful and sensitive manner that trusting relationships are built where values and beliefs are mutually respected.

⚙ REFLECTION 2.2

Reflect upon some of the barriers that inhibit parents from engaging in parental partnership.

» What strategies do you have in place to support this?

» What further strategies could you develop to engage and support parents to participate in their toddlers' learning?

» How can the PEAL materials, provided through peal.org, further support your development and engagement in partnership with parents?

» Reflect upon your understanding of professional boundaries and how this impacts upon your role as an EYPT.

Family, home and environmental factors

In order to support toddlers' wellbeing, EYPTs need to understand the family, home situation and environmental factors that impact upon a toddler's growth, development and learning. The immediate environment in which toddlers and their families live is dependent upon many key factors. These include housing and living conditions, safe and stimulating environment, lifestyle choices of parents and demographics of the community. The impact of these key factors upon toddlers is influential to the quality of life for a toddler and their wellbeing. This can be 'both immediate and long term; growing up in poor or overcrowded housing has been found to have a lasting impact upon a child's health and well-being throughout their life' (Harker, 2006). This is an important consideration as a majority of toddlers spend a considerable amount of time within the home environment.

Environmental factors

Housing

The environmental factors and differences within housing and the impact these have upon toddlers' wellbeing are wide and varied, as the surrounding infrastructure and accessibility to the range of community services and facilities can vary greatly depending upon the environment, local authority/municipality and community provision. For example, the impact will be different for a young family in a rural setting where the community is sparse and spread out, to a family new to a busy suburban community or a family living in temporary or poor housing. EYPTs need to be aware of the living conditions of toddlers and their families in order to be able to provide appropriate support and know what provision is available.

Property types

There is a range of different housing available for families; these can be found in the table below. Families may live in these on their own, with their extended family or share with other people.

Table 2.1 Property types

Detached house	A house that stands alone with no other structure adjoining or attached to it.
Semi-detached house	A house that is attached only on one side to another property.
Terrace	A row of houses that are attached to each other.
Flat, studio flat, apartment	A self-contained house which is part of a building structure with shared access and communal areas, such as gardens.
Refuge accommodation	A safe house for women and their families who are escaping violence and abuse, usually away from the area that they live in.
Temporary accommodation	This is housing provided on a temporary basis for families who have become homeless and they may be placed in a 'bed and breakfast' or hotel room. This is only a temporary resolution until a more permanent solution is found.
Maisonette	A self-contained house which is part of a larger house, with its own separate entrance.
Bungalow	A house that has no stairs and is ground storey only.
Tied housing	This is housing that comes with the job. Caretakers in schools and reverends may have this kind of housing.

Cottage	A period house usually found in the countryside.
Mobile housing – caravans/ trailers, houseboats	This might be a prefabricated home that is able to be moved from place to place, or a boat that has been adapted for living in.

↻ REFLECTION 2.3

Reflect upon the three identified property types of housing and the range of conditions that can affect a toddler's health and wellbeing:

» Period cottage

» High-rise flat

» Houseboat

Identify the positive and negative factors of living in each of these three different property types.

Homes may be owner-occupied by the family, mortgaged, a co-operative or shared ownership. They may also be non-owner occupied, which are privately rented, or social housing where families rent from the local authority/municipality or a housing association.

The condition and circumstances that the housing is in can have a 'direct impact on family income, which in turn significantly affects children's life chances' (Harker, 2006). Harker identifies that housing affects five key areas of children's life chances: 'health and emotional well-being, safety and security, educational attainment, childhood and adult aspirations, income and occupation'.

The impact of the toddlers' housing upon their health and wellbeing is often exacerbated by other problems such as illness, respiratory infections, behavioural difficulties and low academic achievement. These are often not necessarily attributed to their housing conditions. Researchers (Harker, 2006; Marmot, 2010; Mullins, Western and Broadbent, 2001; WHO, 2008) have identified links between living conditions and children's life chances. It is therefore important as EYPTs that an understanding of toddlers' home circumstances is tactfully acquired and supporting provision made within the setting.

♻ REFLECTION 2.4

Consider how your setting's policies and provision support toddlers in the following key areas:

» Health and emotional wellbeing

» Safety and security

» Educational attainment

» Childhood and adult aspirations

» Income and occupation

Housing conditions

There are many differing housing conditions that have an impact on toddlers' healthy growth and development. The standard of living will vary considerably and will influence the life chances and outcomes for each family. Income is directly and indirectly significant in the type of housing that the family has access to. Research into household income identified that workless households are clearly connected with poverty (Harker, 2006). This in turn impacts upon toddlers' future economic wellbeing.

Noise pollution within the home and external environment can be detrimental within toddlers' daily lives. This can include disrupted sleep patterns, constant noise such as transport, industrial machinery and neighbours, and overcrowding resulting in a busy, overstimulating environment. Households that are overcrowded can be an indicator of poverty where toddlers may experience issues relating to physical and mental health, such as stress and anxiety. In addition, long term noise pollution can have an effect on children's hearing and mental health. 'For example, persistent socio-economic pressures are recognized risks to mental health for individuals and communities. The clearest evidence is associated with indicators of poverty, including low levels of education' (WHO, 2016).

Poorly-maintained properties result in unsafe and unhygienic living conditions, such as damp and mould, infestation, inadequate heating, lack of basic facilities and poor ventilation. These all impact upon toddlers' physical and mental health. Toddlers who live in poor housing conditions are at a higher risk of respiratory conditions such as asthma.

Living in an area with a high crime rate can affect the mental health and long term behaviour of children: 'Evidence shows that problem behaviour is more prevalent among children living in poor housing...such difficulties in childhood may manifest themselves later in offending behaviour' (Harker, 2006).

The ability to access essential amenities and facilities within the community is vital in supporting the family and toddlers' wellbeing. Families experiencing financial hardship may find difficulty in accessing amenities and facilities due to their geographical location, distance and access to 'education and care provision and professionals, medical and healthcare facilities and professionals, shops and public services and transportation' (Sutherland and Mukadam, 2018). Families without their own transportation may find accessing services difficult, due to distance, lack of accessible public transport and cost. A potential barrier to accessing the local amenities and facilities is that they may not be within reasonable walking distance from their home.

Disadvantaged families living in rural areas may find transportation difficult, costly and isolating as the distance and time to reach local amenities and facilities is inconvenient and the means is inaccessible. Families living in urban high rise flats may find a lack of access to outdoor facilities. Working households may find factors such as job location and access to transportation, commuting costs and travel time impact upon the quality time that they spend with their toddler.

⟳ REFLECTION 2.5

Tactfully investigate and consider the housing conditions and the environment that the toddlers within your setting are living in, including:

» the type of housing

» condition

» number of people living in the home

» sleeping arrangements

» access to basic facilities, such as hot water and washing amenities, heating and cooking facilities.

What have you learnt about the toddlers' living conditions and how does this help you have a better understanding of the toddlers' needs?

Safe and stimulating

The housing conditions and lifestyle of toddlers and their families will vary greatly and impact upon the opportunities that they have for a safe and simulating home environment. The location of the home and access to local amenities and facilities can either limit or extend toddlers' opportunities for learning and development. Does the local community provide opportunities for safe outdoor play and local facilities such as parks, playgrounds and community toddler groups?

Safety within the home is paramount; however, due to the range of families' socio-economic situations, the levels of safety for toddlers may vary and be compromised through poor housing conditions even though there are regulations such as the Housing Health and Safety Ratings (HHSRS) to evaluate the potential risks and hazards within the home. Families living in poor housing or refuges are more likely to experience accidents or hazards due to the physical conditions of the home (Harker, 2006). This can impact on the play opportunities that toddlers have within the home through the lack of provision, family time and parental engagement, resources, space, living conditions and overcrowding.

> Poor housing conditions have damaging impact upon children's learning...parents in overcrowded homes were less responsive and spoke in less sophisticated ways to their children... Children living in temporary accommodation often face limited space to play and some studies suggest that this can lead to depression or aggressive behavior. (Harker, 2006)

The most common causes of toddlers' accidents in the home are: falls, fires, scalds and burns, suffocating and choking, strangulation, poisoning, drowning and glass-related accidents. Statistics from the Royal Society for the Prevention of Accidents (RoSPA, 2017) state that there are around 6,000 deaths of children each year caused by accidents, with children under five years being the most likely to be involved in an accident within the home.

Partnership with parents is vital as parents, as their first educators, are very influential in their toddlers' future achievements. EYPTs can help parents identify and be aware of the possible risks and take appropriate actions, supporting them in understanding how to create a safe and stimulating environment.

EYPTs can actively support parents in developing the quality of the home environment, with opportunities for early reading and number games, emphasising that learning opportunities do not have to be costly. Time spent engaging with toddlers reading stories, singing rhymes and playing games enables quality parental involvement with little or no cost. Research by Ipsos MORI (2011) on children's views of what wellbeing means to them identified that 'what constitutes a "good day" for children was very simple: time with those they love (friends, family and even pets); creative or sporting activities; being outdoors and having fun'. Therefore, what constituted a good day for children lacked material possessions.

Strategies and tools to support environmental factors

Each local community and has its own unique culture, demographics and environment. What is common in one locality may not be in another. Knowing what, where and how resources and support are available and can be accessed within your locality is important. Ask yourself questions about these strategies and tools. For example, what is on offer from the local authority/municipality in terms of fun days and events, weekly toddler groups, advice and support for housing and food banks? What does the local library offer other than loaning books – story time sessions, toy libraries and other events? What facilities can families access that don't cost money, such as parks, playgrounds, community and children's centres? How can parents be supported and encouraged to engage with their toddler? It is important to provide information, resources and ideas as they can really be helpful for parents and these do not have to cost money, such as encouraging parents to have story times with their toddlers. It might be useful to have dual language story books that parents can borrow if their home language is different to that of the country they are living in, story or rhyme bags that parents can borrow, and to let parents know what stories and rhymes their toddler prefers in the setting.

The following is an example of how these questions can be used to support toddlers and their families:

	Evidence: What evidence do you need? What have you found out?	Action: What actions have you taken? How will you use the knowledge and information gained?
What activities, events and local visits are available for parents to access within your locality?	The local library lends books and toys out to families. The local authority/ municipality holds 'stay and play' sessions for families under 5 or free activity events during the holidays.	Information leaflets on library and session times on the setting's parent notice board or on website. Information leaflets on the 'stay and play' sessions and events on the setting's parent notice board or on website.

Housing and conditions

	Evidence	Action
If a family requires support do you know who they can contact?		
If you have a concern about poor housing conditions who do you contact?		
What amenities and facilities are available for the family to access within your locality? Where do you keep the information? How often is this updated?		

Safe and stimulating

	Evidence	Action
What activities, events and local visits are available for parents to access within your locality? For example – parks and playgrounds, local and community events, library.		
How can you encourage parents to take family time to talk to their toddler?		
How can you encourage story time with parents and their toddlers?		
What resources, events and story times does your local library offer?		
How can you encourage parental partnership and engagement? What PEAL resources are available to help?		
What safety information can you provide to parents? Who can you contact for advice? For example – the fire brigade, which provides information and carries out checks in homes.		
How can you encourage play opportunities within the home?		

Family

Demographics of family and lifestyle

An awareness of the key role that demographics, lifestyle and the geographical location play in supporting toddlers' wellbeing provides EYPTs with a better understanding of the diversity and issues facing families accessing the setting. This enables EYPTs to diversify the setting's provision to better meet the toddler and their family's needs.

Families may have difficulty accessing local facilities where the home language varies from the country/community they live in. Strategies to support this need to be identified to enable families to fully engage within the setting and community. Family backgrounds may vary according to individual experiences, culture, mobility and socio-economic status. The family's standard of living and income is an integral part in determining whether a family experience absolute or relative poverty.

Gaining access to local authority/municipality data sets and statistics will provide information regarding household size, income, deprivation, homelessness and ethnicity data of families living within the locality. This will help provide an understanding of the families accessing the setting. Making links with other settings and community groups – such as health centres, schools, children's centres, community and voluntary organisations – can help build a picture of the needs and provision within the locality. This can then inform setting policies and development of future provision.

⟳ REFLECTION 2.6

Investigate the demographics of the toddlers within your setting. What do demographics of your locality look like in relation to:

» household size

» income

» deprivation

» homelessness

» ethnicity

» languages spoken?

Considering the findings, what have you learnt about the locality?

How does this impact upon your setting's provision? Do you need to make any changes or adapt the provision?

There are a wide range of lifestyle choices that parents make that influence the overall wellbeing of toddlers. However, the following involuntary factors can be detrimental and put toddlers' wellbeing at risk:

- Disability

- Mental Health

- Addictions such as drug abuse, alcoholism and smoking

- Domestic violence

- Medical and health issues

- Child abuse

- Bullying and intimidation

- Bereavement

- Homelessness

- Divorce and separation

The role of the EYPT is to support the facilitation of appropriate information sharing with key services, to encourage a close working relationship and trust between services and the family to ensure the right provision is accessed. EYPTs need to understand and provide appropriate activities, targets and emotional support for toddlers experiencing any of the above. This needs to be tailored to the specific needs of the toddler and their family. Support may come in various forms: informal, through extended family, friends and neighbours; semi-formal through community, voluntary and charity groups; and formal, through government and local authority/ municipality services.

Strategies and tools to support the family

	Evidence	Action
What support groups or early intervention groups are available for parents facing difficulties such as domestic violence or isolation?		
What different charities are operating within the locality and what support do they offer?		
What are the current issues facing the community and how are they impacting upon the families?		
What main languages are spoken within the setting? What strategies are being used to value, recognise and support the different languages within the setting?		

Health of the family

The health of the family and parents will affect the toddler's wellbeing, especially with issues such as long-term illness and hospitalisation, mental health and disabilities. Access to differing health services may vary in relation to geographical location and locality and intervention funding. The continuity that the setting provides for the toddler in a time of stress and uncertainty provides a respite and emotional support.

♻ REFLECTION 2.7

Reflect upon the needs of the families in the setting:

» Are there any health issues or disabilities within the family that you know of that could impact upon the toddler's wellbeing?

» How can the setting sensitively and appropriately support the family?

EYPTs' experiences, reflections and strategies from England, Norway and Spain

ENGLAND

Kathryn Hogarth from Kew, Mortlake, Barnes and East Sheen Children's Centres, Achieving for Children, London

When a child starts at an early years setting, it can be daunting for everyone. It is vital that practitioners are welcoming, open and available to speak to the parents about their thoughts and ideas. As practitioners, we may see the children for long hours during the day, but parents know their children best. Having parents and practitioners working together is mutually beneficial, and this combined knowledge can be so helpful when thinking about the next steps in a child's development. Building these relationships takes time and, with technology playing a huge part in how we share information with parents, we need to make opportunities to have face-to-face conversations and let parents know that their input is valued.

Carrying the mantel of the 'expert' can be a slippery slope. While parents need to know that you are a knowledgeable, experienced professional, you do not want to discourage them from engaging in a conversation by using lots of jargon. Take a minute to think about the information you share with parents. What does EYFS stand for? (Early Years Foundation Stage.) What do we mean by ESOL and SEND? (English for Speakers of Other Languages and Special Educational Needs and Disabilities.) Would you understand it if you weren't immersed in it every day? We have been thinking about the language we use with both the children and their parents, as well as the information presented around the setting. We have reduced the amount of words on a lot of our displays, and focus on key phrases, pictures and easy-to-access leaflets. By request, we have made little booklets for do-it-at-home activities and recipes, as parents were often asking how the play dough was made or what toys are best for certain ages. We are focusing on the setting–home relationship, and thinking of ways to make it stronger.

It is important to think about the children's wellbeing, and the wellbeing of their parents, carers and siblings. If early intervention is needed then the trusting relationship that has been built can be vital in helping the family access support offered by other professionals. The less pressure the parents are under, the more positive and supportive they can be with their children. We want children to thrive academically but, if their physical and emotional needs are not being met, it makes it harder for them to focus and develop.

When a family has their first child, they are 'thrown into a whole new world'. If a family has never had contact with an early years setting before it is unlikely they will know what funding in available. Settings need to make it clear on their advertising/marketing leaflets if they take children on funded places and accept childcare vouchers. It also helps if the setting makes contact with their Early Years Advisor, the local Family Information Service, and the local children's centre to ensure that good information sharing is happening, and all the opportunities for advertising and promotion are being utilised.

Working alongside the family, respecting their culture and beliefs, and inviting them in to the setting will support the development of a mutually beneficial relationship. It is a practitioner's job to embrace and celebrate these beliefs, working to support and improve the children's wellbeing through new opportunities and experiences.

NORWAY

Liv Hjertø from Sandvedhaugen Barnehage[1], Sandnes Kommune, Sandnes

When we used the toddler wellbeing audit tool [the strategies and tools to support…within this book], we decided that our primary focus would be on the familiarisation process and on the role of parents and key persons in that process. The staff in the project groups had a particular focus on assessing our practice with respect to the attachment theory (John Bowlby, 2008) and the Circle of Security (The Circle of Security Network, 2015). The COS is a user-friendly model for analysing and interpreting children's actions, emotions and needs in order to guide parents in supporting development during the provision of care. It was launched in 1998 and has since been developed by the four clinicians Bert Powell, Glen Cooper, Kent Hoffman and Bob Marvin. The aim of the model is to ensure that the child develops a secure attachment to their parents. We use this model as a tool in guiding the staff, as an aid when working to ensure that insecure children develop a secure attachment at the pre-school, during the familiarisation period for all young children, and for preventive purposes. We have worked to ensure that the practitioners are there and available to provide support, comfort and encouragement when the children need it. The reason why we decided to use familiarisation and attachment as a starting point was fundamental in ensuring that the

---

1   The Norwegian term *barnehage* is a literal translation of the German word *kindergarten*, and is used for early years settings for children age one to five.

children have the conditions they need to be able to open up, explore and develop in the pre-school environment.

We have also reflected on what the attachment theory and the COS mean as regards the roles of adult and key person during the familiarisation period and how we can adapt and change the roles of adult and key person to facilitate children's attachment in the pre-school. We have found that providing parents with information on the COS and attachment theories is important. It helps to give them a tool with which they can support and reassure their child during the familiarisation process. During the year, we have had a greater focus on the collaboration between the parents and staff during the familiarisation period, and on how the pre-school and parents can help each other to give the children a secure attachment to the secondary care persons in the pre-school. We have found that the staff have become more aware that establishing a secure sense of attachment for a young child in the pre-school takes time, and that it is important to give the child this time. The staff have given the children more time to familiarise themselves and feel secure, and they are now listening to the children's voices and expressions more consciously. We believe this is reflected in the children's improved wellbeing and enjoyment. We realised that the toddler wellbeing audit tool worked well in relation to the role of adult. We saw an improvement in wellbeing and a sense of mastery amongst both the children and the adults.

The tool was useful when meeting parents. We talked to them about their children's voices and expressions, explaining that it is natural for a young child to cry when their mother or father has brought them to pre-school and has to leave them. We had a good dialogue with parents concerning the importance of meeting the emotional needs of children for reassurance, support and comfort. We have previously seen that diversion has often been used as a tactic by both parents and staff when a child cries. We now use the COS in all our staff training, in discussions with guardians and when guiding staff. The groups that applied the ToWe Project and the toddler wellbeing audit tool received excellent feedback from the parents in the user survey, particularly regarding their views on the familiarisation process.

At our pre-school, we traditionally have two reviews [parent–teacher conferences] with parents every year. The issues covered in these reviews vary. After reading the wellbeing manual (Sutherland and Mukadam, 2018), we reflected on the content and issues covered during these parent reviews. We realised that we had to become even better at taking the time to get to know the families and show a deeper interest in the families' situations, including their home life, family circumstances, health and finances. We simply had to be brave and bring up subjects that we had previously avoided, perhaps because we have found that both we and the parents have found it unpleasant to discuss sensitive issues. On occasions, we have considered these to be subjects and issues that are brought up by the public health nurse at the medical centre and therefore of little relevance to discuss in a pre-school. We now realise that the pre-school can benefit from having a greater insight into these factors in order to meet the child and the family with understanding and respect, and to gain a deeper understanding of the needs of each family and child. In this way, we can better align the pre-school with the needs of the individual children, thereby helping to improve wellbeing. We have reflected on these issues within the project and the working group. We have considered the creation of a help form for the teachers with set questions to be asked during the parent reviews, where topics such as home life, health, family circumstances and finance are brought up. We realise that these can be sensitive issues for the parents and it is important that they are brought up in a sensitive and respectful manner. We also realise that consideration must be given on a case-by-case basis as to whether it is appropriate to ask questions concerning the family and home environment during reviews. We concluded that we should develop a template for reviews that outlines topics to be brought up and that we should discuss issues within topics that we believe would be natural to bring up with individual parents.

Pre-schools are an important arena for helping to ensure that families and children receive the appropriate help and support when it is needed. It can sometimes be appropriate for this support to be provided by other support services within the municipality, such as the Educational Psychological Counselling Service (PPT), the child welfare service, medical centre, and so on. A high proportion of children of pre-school age in Norway now have a pre-school place. The pre-school is therefore an important arena for mediating contact with these support services and an important collaboration partner for guardians in contact with other support services. The pre-school often acts as a link both between support services and between support services and guardians, and we are dependent on a strong dialogue with guardians as well as a relationship based on trust and security.

One of the support services in the municipality is the Centre for Multilingual Children and Adolescents (*Senter for flerspråklige barn og unge*). They have developed a number of forms to be used as aids in the pre-school's interaction with multilingual children and their families. For example, there is a form with questions and topics that might be appropriate to discuss during the first review. We realise that we have been a little wary of bringing up matters that we think may be sensitive for parents. We now have experience that demonstrates that many parents appreciate having a good discussion covering sensitive issues with us. Experience suggests that the key to a good, productive review concerning sensitive issues is more about the way in which we talk about such issues rather than the issues themselves.

After using the wellbeing tool, we saw the need to change and adjust the content of the first meeting with new parents. We had previously talked a lot during these meetings about the history of the pre-school, the number of groups, the number of children, the duties of the management, the pre-school's planning documents, etc. These meetings are now used more to tell the parents about the COS and attachment in order to ensure they are best-placed to help their child during the familiarisation period at the pre-school. We have a very engaged group of parents who want the best for their children. In recent years, we have observed what we might interpret as insecurity in some parents – insecurity that can, as we have seen, also affect the child. With the staff and management helping to give parents a greater insight into how they can support their child during the familiarisation process and working more closely with them during this process, we are enabling parents to help give their child secure attachments and wellbeing at the pre-school, something that can in turn make the parents more secure. A child's parents are its primary attachment persons and the pre-school's most important partners for giving the child a secure attachment to the pre-school. As pre-school teachers and staff, we also see it as our task to reassure the parents.

SPAIN

Natàlia Turmo and Sílvia Turmo from Petita Escola, Barcelona, Cataluña

School and family do not act independently from each other; instead, we both have to work hand in hand and make parallel progress. Teachers and parents are the adults that support children and act as the safe base from which they venture forth and learn about the world. We are the safe haven where they find affection and the model that accompanies them as they learn about themselves and how to manage their emotions.

At Petita Escola, we think about families in general, but also each family in particular, and about their specific situations in order to understand each child better.

The reality of our school, in terms of its environment and housing, is quite uniform. Most of the families live in the neighbourhood, where there are many parks, shops and schools. They all live in decent homes that are spacious and safe. Most of the families are upper-middle class professionals who earn a good living.

The most variable factor in the school's families is the kind of activities, stimuli or interactions the children receive outside of school. That is, the quantity and quality of time they spend with their families.

At school, we think that we can do a lot in this sense, and this is why we have formulas for connecting with the families in different ways. Below we have classified some of the avenues of communication and interaction with the families, but they are often interconnected. In fact, we can use any time or place we meet with parents to listen to and learn from them, to help them, to inform them or to make them feel part of the family we try to create at Petita Escola.

- *Listening to families; welcoming opinions, suggestions and feedback; and learning from parents.* We like to listen to parents' comments. We highly value their constructive outside perspective. Midway through the academic year, we send home a brief questionnaire where we ask them to highlight the strong and weak points of certain aspects of the school. The comments we collect anonymously are essential to improving the school.

- *Informing families.* We offer families the chance to hold as many personal meetings with their child's teacher throughout the academic year as they want. We hold quarterly meetings with all the families in the class group in order to keep them abreast of general information and give them the chance to meet the other parents in the group to share questions, concerns and topics of mutual interest. Each child has their own personal date book in which we share basic daily information, as well as an individual portfolio where we document their development and learning through written texts, photographs, cut-outs, etc. The families receive information on their child's development at the beginning and end of the school year. We post photographs and texts from each group on the school intranet weekly.

- *Getting the families involved by encouraging them to participate in the school to which they belong.* We have a range of extracurricular activities with families (music, psycho-motor skills, theatre). The families also participate in many of the festivals and celebrations held at school.

- *Guiding, orienting, advising, inspiring or serving as a model for families.* We encourage families to participate in university projects. In recent months, we have been involved in a project called 'Parenthood and Development', which is studying the influence of interactions between parents and children, specifically the way they play together, on their motor, linguistic and cognitive development. The families appreciate this kind of opportunity.

The attitude of the educators, the materials we use at school, the layout of the furniture in the classroom and the kinds of activities we do at school can serve as a model or inspiration for families.

The school also serves as a point of contact between the families and specialised centres like Child Development and Early Care Centres (CDIAPs) and Educational Psychology Advisement Teams (EAPs) or private centres. The school also works with a team of psychologists and psycho-motor experts whom the families may talk to if they need advice or help.

These ties created with the parents of the school help strengthen each party's knowledge of the child. We enrich each other, and this has direct effects on the children's wellbeing.

Somehow, the bonds created with the families are the avenue through which this wellbeing which we so keenly seek and ensure at school reaches the children's family environment as well. The ToWe Project is not confined to the four walls of the school but instead spreads through our relationships with the families.

Conclusion

This chapter has investigated the key factors and areas that impact upon toddlers' family, home and environmental factors and the importance of working with parents to build positive relations in order to effectively communicate and support toddlers and their families. The chapter has explored how environmental factors such as housing condition and property types can seriously impact upon toddlers' and their families' health and life chances. It is important that EYPTs emphasise the importance of how to provide and develop a safe and stimulating environment for toddlers. EYPTs can use the strategies and tools identified within this chapter to develop and enhance their own knowledge and understanding of the home and wider environment and how this can be used to develop, support and access provision. Understanding the demographic of the locality and family situations is important in tailoring the setting's provision and providing personalised support. EYPTs' experiences, reflections and strategies were shared from England, Norway and Spain. This dimension provides EYPTs with underpinning knowledge and family background that recognises the complexities that family life and situations have on toddlers' wellbeing. This provides the foundations and building blocks for the other dimensions covered in the chapters which follow.

References

Bowlby, J. (2008) *Attachment*. New York, NY: Basic Books.

Children Act 1989, c. 2. Accessed 18 January 2017 at www.legislation.gov.uk/ukpga/1989/41/section/2

DfE (2014) *Statutory Framework for the Early Years Foundation Stage*. Accessed 18 January 2017 at www.foundationyears.org.uk/files/2014/07/EYFS_framework_from_1_September_2014__with_clarification_note.pdf

DfE (2017) *Statutory Framework for the Early Years Foundation Stage: Setting the Standards for Learning, Development and Care for Children from Birth to Five*. Accessed 29 January 2018 at https://www.foundationyears.org.uk/files/2017/03/EYFS_STATUTORY_FRAMEWORK_2017.pdf

DoH (2009) *Healthy Child Programme: Pregnancy and the first five years of life*. Accessed 18 January 2017 at https://www.gov.uk/government/uploads/system/uploads/attachment_data/file/167998/Health_Child_Programme.pdf

Harker, L. (2006) *Chance of a lifetime: The impact of bad housing on children's lives*. Accessed 4 January 2017 at https://england.shelter.org.uk/__data/assets/pdf_file/0016/39202/Chance_of_a_Lifetime.pdf

Ipsos MORI (2011) *Children's Well-being in UK, Sweden and Spain: The Role of Inequality and Materialism*. Accessed 4 January 2017 at https://www.ipsos-mori.com/DownloadPublication/1441_sri-unicef-role-of-inequality-and-materialism-june-2011.pdf

Marmot, M. (2010) *Strategic Review of Health Inequalities in England Post-2010. Fair Society, Healthy Lives: The Marmot Review Executive Summary*. Accessed 4 January 2017 at www.parliament.uk/documents/fair-society-healthy-lives-full-report.pdf

Mullins, P., Western, J. and Broadbent, B. (2001) *The links between housing and nine key socio cultural factors: A review of the evidence positioning paper.* Australian Housing and Urban Research Institute Queensland Research Centre. Accessed 13 February 2017 at https://www.ahuri.edu.au/__data/assets/pdf_file/0018/2736/AHURI_Positioning_Paper_No4_Links_between_housing_and_nine_key_socio_cultural_factors.pdf

Public Health England (2015) *Rapid Review to Update Evidence for the Healthy Child Programme 0–5.* Accessed 18 January 2017 at https://www.gov.uk/government/uploads/system/uploads/attachment_data/file/429740/150520RapidReviewHealthyChildProg_UPDATE_poisons_final.pdf

RoSPA (The Royal Society for the Prevention of Accidents) (2017) *Facts & Figures in Home Safety.* Accessed 1 March 2017 at www.rospa.com/home-safety/advice/general/facts-and-figures

Sutherland, H. and Mukadam, Y. (2018) *Toddlers' Wellbeing Manual.* ToWe Project 2015–2018. Accessed 30 November 2017 at www.toddlerswellbeing.eu

The Circle of Security Network (2015) *The Circle of Security.* Accessed 13 February 2018 at http://circleofsecuritynetwork.org/the_circle_of_security.html

UNICEF UK (1989) *A summary of the UN Convention on the Rights of the Child.* Accessed 14 March 2017 at https://www.unicef.org.uk/wp-content/uploads/2010/05/UNCRC_summary-1.pdf

Wheeler, H. and Connor, J. (2006) *Parents, Early Years and Learning (PEAL).* London: National Children's Bureau.

WHO (World Health Organisation) (2008) *The Commission calls for closing the health gap in a generation: Health equity through action on the social determinants of health.* Accessed 4 January 2017 at http://apps.who.int/iris/bitstream/10665/43943/1/9789241563703_eng.pdf

WHO (World Health Organisation) (2016) *Mental health: Strengthening our response.* Accessed 1 March 2017 at www.who.int/mediacentre/factsheets/fs220/en

CHAPTER 3

HEALTH OF TODDLERS

Helen Sutherland and Yasmin Mukadam

'Every child has the right to the best possible health. Governments must provide good quality health care, clean water, nutritious food, and a clean environment and education on health and well-being so that children can stay healthy. Richer countries must help poorer countries achieve this.'

———————————— *(UNICEF UK, 1989)* ————————————

Introduction

This chapter will look at what constitutes the health of toddlers and how this impacts upon their wellbeing. This will include toddlers' physical and mental health, childhood illnesses, toddlers' needs and abilities and factors that may inhibit wellbeing. The use of health checks and immunisations to maintain toddlers' health and wellbeing will be explored. The chapter will consider current strategies and interventions that will support the development of a healthy and happy toddler. Reflective opportunities will be used to develop understanding and awareness of toddlers' health and how this supports wellbeing. Reflections and experiences from early years practitioners and teachers (EYPTs) of how they support the health of toddlers in England and Spain will be provided.

Physical and mental health

Understanding and supporting both the physical and mental health of toddlers is an important role for the EYPT, as there are many different factors that impact upon this. 'Health is a state of complete physical, mental and social well-being and not merely the absence of disease or infirmity' (WHO, 2014a).

Physical health relates to the wellbeing of the body, both internally and externally. It is about being able to fully engage with all daily activities and the achievement of the expected developmental milestones.

Mental health is the wellbeing of the mind and is a state of emotional and psychological wellbeing, concerned with the ability to cope with the normal stresses of everyday life. It is about enabling toddlers to manage and understand the range of emotions that they may face and develop strategies and emotional resilience to cope with these feelings. By supporting the good mental health of toddlers, it provides them with the ability to cope with the daily difficulties and issues that they may face.

Physical and mental health are linked closely together as toddlers learn to regulate and manage their feelings which may be exhibited through physical behaviour. If a toddler is tired, frustrated or upset this can manifest in a range of emotions and behaviours that they do not yet understand and it is the role then of the EYPT to support and help them understand and regulate these strong feelings.

The World Health Organisation (WHO) is an international organisation that researches a wide range of health issues and concerns, providing data, statistics and strategies which inform the United Nations and support the creation of a world health agenda.

The WHO supports governments to formulate policies and initiatives to promote families' and toddlers' wellbeing. Through their research, they provide recommendations, guidance, standards, statistics and frameworks on a range of world health issues and concerns. The All Party Parliamentary Group on Wellbeing Economics (2014) identified the importance of the development of wellbeing within four key areas. This was highlighted by the Chief Medical Officer within her 2013 annual report (All Party Parliamentary Group on Wellbeing Economics, 2015) where she cited the WHO's 2010 Global Burden of Disease Study which identified the financial burden and cost of mental ill health on the health system and the government identified initiatives and recommendations to tackle the issue.

Physical health

Toddlers' life experiences are critical as their social and economic situation can have a huge impact upon their health, wellbeing, growth and development, with disadvantaged toddlers being more susceptible to disease, illness and malnutrition. The Marmot Review highlighted that families with higher socio-economic situations have more opportunities to have a healthier life. This then has an impact upon the life chances and opportunities of toddlers who are not within the higher socio-economic group as 'what happens during these early years (starting in the womb) has lifelong effects on many aspects of health and well-being – from obesity, heart disease and mental health, to educational achievement and economic status' (Marmot, 2010).

It is therefore important for EYPTs to be aware and understand what they can do to support toddlers' physical and mental health and what strategies and initiatives they can access and implement to support disadvantaged toddlers.

⟳ REFLECTION 3.1

» What WHO health agendas are you aware of?

» Have a look at the WHO website www.who.int.

» How do you currently support the physical and mental health of toddlers as part of the provision within your setting?

» Identify a factor that impacts upon a toddler's physical health. What can you do to negate this factor?

» Identify a factor that impacts upon a toddler's mental health. What can you do to negate this factor?

» How do your setting's policies and provision reflect current WHO initiatives?

Mental health

Promoting good mental health and wellbeing can positively impact on a person's life by improving health outcomes, life expectancy, productivity and educational and economic outcomes (DoH, 2010).

'At a time when children's mental health is of increasing concern', the Good Child Report (The Children's Society, 2016, p.3) highlights the links between wellbeing and mental health issues and evidence-based practice arising from the Children's Society and New Economics Foundation (NEF)'s adapted model of the Five Ways to Wellbeing (DOH and PHE, 2014a). The New Economics' 'Five Ways to a Happy Childhood' provides a framework for health visitors to use with children and families to promote emotional wellbeing and positive mental health of children.

However, a major growth of interest to improve wellbeing within the education field has been seen in an approach known as 'mindfulness'. The term mindfulness, which is starting to become more widely recognised, was coined by Jon Kabat-Zinn in the late 1990s, who defines it as 'paying attention to your experience from moment to moment' (Kabat-Zinn, 2013, p.18). Research by the WHO (WHO, 2014b) recognised the interrelation between mental health and the topic of mindfulness with the definition 'Mental Health is a state of wellbeing in which every individual recognises his or her own potential, can cope with the normal stresses of life... and is able to make a contribution to her or his community.' The Wellbeing Economics Report (NEF, 2014) identified that the UK had become a national leader in measuring wellbeing, yet wellbeing was not yet being widely used to inform policy. This led to the All-Party Parliamentary Group for Wellbeing Economics (2014) report which set out a key recommendation to introduce mindfulness into the basic training of teachers with the policy area, 'Building personal resources: mindfulness in health and education'.

EYPTs can use a range of techniques with toddlers within the settings with the aim to embed mindfulness within a wellbeing curriculum in order to:

- enhance toddlers' overall health

- support emotional development

- develop resilience

- provide calmness and relaxation techniques

- support behaviour.

The following six mindfulness strategies can be carried out within the daily routine:

1. Mindful walks enable toddlers to become aware of the natural beauty of the outdoor environment around them. They heighten self-awareness of the body through gentle physical movements, offering toddlers moments to pause and use their senses to look at, absorb and engage with nature and the elements.

2. The bell listening exercise can be incorporated into the daily routine. It acts as a gentle reminder for toddlers and practitioners to relax the body and become aware of their breathing. It can be set to chime gently and enables toddlers to stop and listen, with a few moments of breathing, stretching and resting. This is best role modelled by adults working with toddlers.

3. Breathing buddies can be done at any time to help toddlers focus on deep belly breathing. It calms the nervous system and is easy to do (see Table 3.1). This is a useful strategy to encourage rest and sleep routines during the day.

4. Sit and be is a gentle seated practice that practitioners can use daily to help toddlers to feel seated and grounded. It can encourage body awareness and calmness. The practitioner can ask them to notice their feet, resting them on the ground. This then moves upwards to the legs, tummy, arms, shoulders and head, tapping the areas gently and closing their eyes. Gentle music can be played alongside this for a few minutes per day.

5. Smell and Tell enables toddlers to share the sensory experience of looking at, touching and tasting a range of different fruits, vegetables, foods and resources. This supports them to focus on details, using their senses to notice smells, tastes and textures of familiar and new experiences. This engages concentration of the mind to improve learning through play opportunities.

6. Art of Touch provides present moment curiosity and exploration for toddlers using a range of materials and resources within their environment. Toddlers are given objects to explore through touch such as natural resources, artefacts,

feathers, balls, soft toys, and so on. They can explore and be encouraged to express their feelings about the objects and share with others, supporting calmness and exploration through touch.

By enabling wellbeing opportunities for toddlers, EYPTs will themselves develop a present moment awareness and positive state which helps to declutter the brain and to make room for creativity, potentially boosting learning within a calm and relaxed environment.

⟳ REFLECTION 3.2

Identify three changes that can be made within your setting to better support toddlers' wellbeing within the current curriculum. (For example, organising a space called the 'Being Calm' area for sitting and quiet time.)

1.

2.

3.

Table 3.1 provides mindfulness strategies to support toddler wellbeing through the use of the wellbeing framework.

Table 3.1 Link to wellbeing framework

Wellbeing aspect	Activity to embed mindfulness
Toddlers' family, home and environmental factors	*Pause and petal practice*: Work with individual or a group of toddlers to support calmness and relaxation. Give them a fragrant flower to hold in their hand, like jasmine or lavender. Ask them to close their eyes and breathe in the smell through their nose and breathe out through their mouth. *Benefits*: Children focus on breathing and counting the breath in and out, noticing how they feel.
Health of toddlers	*Wiggle, squish and relax*: Children sit or lie on the floor, eyes closed, and then wiggle, squish or relax different parts of the body, for example, squish the toes, squeeze hands together, relax hands on the knees. *Benefits*: Body and mind awareness, children understand the art of 'being present'.

Wellbeing aspect	Activity to embed mindfulness
Setting environment for toddlers	*Heart to heart:* Work in a small group or individual one-to-one time to share and express feelings. A simple way is to encourage toddlers to pay attention to sounds that they can hear. You can use a singing bowl, a bell, musical instruments or sounds using a phone app. They can sit or lie down. Placing their hands on their tummy or heart centre will help them feel calm and develop awareness of their inner and outer experiences. Sharing words about feelings through verbal or picture cues will help toddlers to associate the word with the feeling. *Benefits:* Exploring emotions, noticing own feelings, regulating emotions by being calm.
Toddlers' development and learning	*Moving softly and calmly:* Introduce children to the present moment, introducing opportunities for moving with softness and peacefulness through different environments. For example, a lion hunting through long grass; a frog sitting on a lily leaf; a cat stretching its legs; and a dog wagging its tail. *Benefits:* Body awareness, sharing feelings, encouraging stillness and soft movements, encouraging language, personal, social and emotional development through movement and interactions with others.
Toddlers' voice and expressions	*Jungle walking and talking:* Introduce toddlers to a range of relaxing nature sounds and expressions, with opportunities to explore the natural outdoors, including insects, twigs, birds and trees. Talk about and imitate the sounds, creating their own jungle animal sounds and movements. Create a jungle display. *Benefits:* Helps toddlers connect to the present moment, develop perception, slow down and notice sounds with opportunities to explore and express themselves.
Toddlers' additional languages	*Breathing buddies:* Give each toddler a soft toy and have them lie down on the floor, placing the soft toy on their chest, then belly. Ask them to breathe in and lift the soft toy up with their tummy. Explore a range of rhymes in different languages that reflect the toddlers in the setting. Introduce resources that engage toddlers and enhance language development. For example, 'Hello Around the World' and translation of rhymes such as 'Ladybird, Ladybird'. *Benefits:* Listening to others, sharing, expressing emotions through languages.
Toddlers' mealtimes	*Taste and smell adventure:* Select a range of fragrant fruits and foods which can be shared with toddlers during a snack or mealtime. Introduce them to a range of flavours and smells. Ask them to close their eyes and breathe in the scent, focusing their attention on the taste or the smell. For example, orange peel, apple, bread. Talk with the toddlers about their experiences. *Benefits:* Tuning into experiences, using the senses, focusing the mind through mindful tasting and smelling.

Strategies and tools to support physical and mental health of toddlers

	Evidence	Action
How does your setting promote the physical health of toddlers using physical development? For example, potty training and hygiene routines.		
How does your setting promote the mental health of toddlers using personal, social and emotional development? For example, a healthy expression of their own feelings and regulating and managing their behaviour.		
How does the physical environment of your setting support physical and mental health and wellbeing? What activities do you provide for the release of feelings? For example, a sensory/ calm area, for large gross motor movement to release energy.		

Health and childhood illnesses

The UN Convention on the Rights of the Child, Article 24 (UNICEF, 1989) highlights the aspects that 'every child has a right to the best possible health'. It states that governments must provide children with good quality health resources, such as healthcare services and clean water, to ensure that children stay healthy. This lays strong foundations for their future health and wellbeing.

It is important that EYPTs work in partnership with families and other services to identify, make provision for and support the ongoing health needs of toddlers. Improving mental health and wellbeing is not just the role of the health service but the development of a working partnership between different local authority/municipality services and other organisations, such as housing, education (including early years settings) and employment departments as well as charity and voluntary services (NHS England, 2016). Key initiatives instigated by the UK government are:

- The Healthy Child Programme, which has been ongoing since 2009, for early intervention and supporting the healthy development of children and their families (DoH and DCSF, 2009).

- The Five Year Forward View for Mental Health plan for transforming mental health care in England (NHS England, 2016).

- Nutrition Matters for Early Years is a Public Health Agency (PHA) resource for early years settings providing advice and information on a range of nutritional issues based on current UK government guidance (PHA, 2016).

Childhood illnesses

There are a wide range of childhood illnesses that toddlers may contract in their lives. Specific childhood illnesses are required to be notified to the local authority or health protection team by a Registered Medical Practitioner under the Notification of Infectious Diseases (NOIDs) (Public Health England, 2014).

Some childhood illnesses may cause complications and health issues, such as measles, mumps and rubella. There are also chronic illnesses – those that last for three months or more – such as sickle cell anaemia, asthma and epilepsy, that may impact upon toddlers' health and wellbeing and may not have a cure. These will require specialist input and provision with early years practitioners and teachers needing specific training to provide the right support and strategies to ensure that the toddlers are fully included within the setting and that their medical needs are met. Some childhood illnesses can be prevented through immunisation, while others can be treated. Some chronic illnesses may be genetic/hereditary and others environmental. Below is a list of childhood illnesses, chronic illnesses and health concerns that toddlers may experience:

- Allergies and food allergies
- Asthma
- Cancer and Leukaemia

- Cerebral Palsy
- Chickenpox
- Cold sores

- Congenital heart problems

- Coughs, colds and flu

- Cystic fibrosis

- Diarrhoea and vomiting

- Ear problems – glue ear or ear infection

- Eczema

- Epilepsy

- Febrile seizures/ convulsions

- Fifth disease – slapped cheek syndrome

- Hand, foot and mouth disease

- HIV/AIDS

- Impetigo

- Infestations – head lice, worms

- Kawasaki disease

- Malnutrition

- Maltreatment

- Measles

- Meningitis

- Mumps

- Obesity

- Rubella

- Scabies

- Scarlet fever

- Sickle cell anaemia

- Sleeping disorders

- Tonsillitis

- Whooping cough

(Sutherland and Mukadam, 2018)

ACTIVITY 3.1

Sort the list into the following headings:

» Childhood illnesses

» Chronic illnesses

» Health concerns

Which of these are notifiable?

Look at the Guidance on Infection Control in Schools and Other Childcare Settings (PHA, 2013).

EYPTs need to know what to do in the event that a toddler becomes unwell while in the setting. They will in some cases have specialised training on the policies and procedures for the care of the toddler and administration of any medication (this can only be done if parental/carer permission has been obtained), identification, recording and reporting of the illnesses or health concerns, as well as the infection control measures to be undertaken, and who they are required to contact and notify. It is a statutory requirement under the Early Years Foundation Stage (EYFS) that early years providers 'must have a procedure, discussed with parents and/or carers, for responding to children who are ill or infectious, take necessary steps to prevent the spread of infection, and take appropriate action if children are ill' (DfE, 2017). The infection control measures they may need to implement are the wearing of disposable gloves and aprons, washing of hands, cleaning of the environment and how to deal with bodily fluids such as vomit, blood or urine.

The PHA provides advice and guidance on how to prevent the spread of infection and the recommended time toddlers should be away from the setting if they have an infection or childhood illness, such as skin infection, rashes, diarrhoea and vomiting, respiratory infections and other infections including meningitis and mumps (PHA, 2013).

Strategies and tools to support childhood illnesses

	Evidence	Action
What are your setting's identification and reporting policies and procedures for childhood illness?		
How do you make provision for the inclusion of chronic illnesses such as sickle cell anaemia, allergies, asthma and epilepsy?		
What procedure do you have in place for the notification of infections and illnesses?		

What infection control measures/procedures do you have in your setting? Good hygiene practices.		
What are the notifiable diseases and who do you contact? Notifying agencies and parents – Notification of Infectious Diseases (NOIDs)		

Needs and abilities

EYPTs need to have an understanding of each toddler's individual learning needs and how they can support these needs further. It is important the toddler's development is supported and challenged to enable them to reach their full potential, taking into consideration their background, abilities, dispositions and interests. Each toddler is unique and will develop and learn at their own rate. Chapters 4 and 5 will address how the setting and learning environment can be used and adapted to meet toddlers' wellbeing through a flexible and adaptable environment.

The United Nations Convention on the Rights of the Child identified in Article 23 that 'a child with a disability has the right to live a full and decent life with dignity and, as far as possible, independence and to play an active part in the community. Governments must do all they can to support disabled children and their families' (UNICEF UK, 1989). This is demonstrated through the Special Educational Needs and Disability Code of Practice which provides the statutory requirements for all schools and early years settings to adhere to. EYPTs need to have an ethos of inclusion and equality of opportunity to enable toddlers to fully engage making provision so that they can achieve their full potential (DoH and DfE, 2014).

♻ REFLECTION 3.3

Review and reflect on your setting's provision, policies, the environment and resources and how they contribute and support the inclusion of toddlers' individual needs and abilities.

» How does your setting embrace toddlers with any particular needs and/or disabilities as part of the setting's community?

Strategies and tools to support needs and abilities

	Evidence	Action
What resource and materials do you have that support toddlers' individual needs and interests? For example: Interests – dinosaurs, favourite stories and rhymes. Needs – bi/multi-lingual books, spring-loaded scissors.		
How do you work in partnership with the parents to further support toddlers' needs and abilities?		
How does your setting value, respect and welcome toddlers' languages and culture?		
How does your setting support inclusive practice?		
What skills do your staff already have and what additional training might they need?		

Factors that inhibit wellbeing

There are a range of factors that can inhibit a toddler's wellbeing and development, and 'families subject to a higher-than-average risk of experiencing multiple problems include those:

- living in social housing
- with a young mother or young father
- where the mother's main language is not English
- where the parents are not co-resident
- where one or both parents grew up in care.'

(DoH and DCSF, 2009, p.17)

A combination of these can result in children being at risk of poor educational and social outcomes (DoH and DCSF, 2009).

There are a range of biological/genetic and environmental factors that can impact upon the health and wellbeing of toddlers. These can include:

> maternal diseases during the anti-natal period, genetic/hereditary diseases, such as, haemophilia and muscular dystrophy, environment and environmental teratogens such as toxins and chemicals, legal and illegal drugs, foetal alcohol syndrome, alcohol, smoking, obesity, nutrition, maltreatment, abuse and foster care. (Sutherland and Mukadam, 2018)

Other factors also include housing conditions that impact on physical and mental health, bereavement, divorce and separation and chronic illnesses and disabilities.

♻ REFLECTION 3.4

Linking back to Chapter 2 – consider how the family, home and environmental factors relate to the listed factors that inhibit toddlers' wellbeing.

Strategies and tools to support factors that may inhibit wellbeing

	Evidence	Action
What provision, strategies, activities and experiences does your setting have to support the following factors that inhibit a toddler's wellbeing: • bereavement • chronic illness • childhood illness • obesity • housing and home environment?		
What other strategies, activities and experiences can you develop to support these factors? For example, therapeutic and sensory activities, calm and quiet spaces, stories and books and parental information.		

Health checks

Within the first five years of a child's life they will undergo health checks to monitor their growth and development in relation to meeting the developmental milestones for their expected age range. It is the role of the health professionals to work with families to review and advise on any concerns or needs that have been identified. They will review:

- gross motor skills

- fine motor skills

- vision

- communication

- hearing

- social skills

- behaviour

- safety.

Other areas that could be reviewed are:

- sleeping patterns and habits

- eating

- oral health.

Percentile charts are used to monitor weight, height, and head circumference to check that they are within a similar percentage. Early intervention can then be assessed and implemented for any specific conditions, concerns or needs identified through the monitoring process. This enables appropriate provision and strategies to be put in place. The Healthy Child Programme (DoH and DCSF, 2009) introduced the two to two-and-a-half-year review to ensure that toddlers' development is monitored to ensure close collaborative working between health professionals and early years practitioners. This programme also introduced the prenatal 28-week check, new birth review, six to eight week review, one-year review, two to two-and-a-half-year review (DoH and DCSF, 2009).

The two-year progress check was introduced in 2012 (NCB, 2012) to review toddlers' development within the EYFS, focusing mainly on the three prime areas for development and learning. This is carried out by EYPTs who work closely with the toddler and have a unique understanding of their development and learning between their second and third birthday. 'This progress check must identify the child's strengths and any areas where the child's progress is less than expected' (DfE, 2017). The two-year progress check and Healthy Child Programme (HCP) two to two-and-a-half year review 'should inform each other and support integrated working' (DfE, 2017). The concept of an integrated review at two is being explored by the DoH and DfE.

Immunisations

Immunisations are used to prevent diseases and are given at intervals throughout a toddler's life to help prevent or reduce the chances of catching diseases. These are usually given in the form of vaccinations under a country's health programme to build up antibodies to diseases. An immunisation schedule is discussed with parents by health professionals raising awareness of illnesses and disease that can be vaccinated against. These schedules identify what vaccinations happen when and those that require additional booster vaccination to maintain immunity. Different countries will have their own immunisation regime for the vaccination of different diseases. It is very important that staff are up to date with their own immunisations.

ACTIVITY 3.2

Identify what diseases are immunised against within your home country and when these happen.

Immunisation	What age are children vaccinated?		
Diphtheria	8 weeks old	12 weeks old	16 weeks old
Tetanus			
Whooping cough			
Polio			
Hib (Haemophilus influenza type b)			

---

cont.

Immunisation	What age are children vaccinated?		
Measles, Mumps and Rubella (MMR)			
Men B (meningitis and septicaemia)			
Rotavirus (highly infectious stomach bug)			
Children's flu vaccine			
Others vaccinations…			

Look for the answers for the UK at:

www.nhs.uk/Conditions/vaccinations/pages/vaccination-schedule-age-checklist.aspx (NHS Choices, 2017)

⟳ REFLECTION 3.5

Reflect upon how your setting carries out reviews of toddlers' progress in relation to learning and development.

» How and when do you link with the health professionals?

» What reactions do you need to be aware of for toddlers in your setting that have just been vaccinated?

Reflect upon how you work with your local health professionals and what information and support can they provide.

Strategies and tools to support health checks and immunisations

	Evidence	Action
How does your setting follow up and provide for toddlers' needs in relation to the two-year progress check and the HCP review?		
Do you know who your local health care team are and how to contact them?		
How does the setting engage with families in facilitating toddlers' two-year progress check and the HCP review?		
What strategies are in place in your setting to check that health care checks and immunisations are up to date?		
What systems are in place within your setting to record toddlers' vaccinations?		
Do you check that all staff are up to date with their immunisations?		

EYPTs' experiences, reflections and strategies from England and Spain

ENGLAND

Janette Barber from Heathfield Children's Centre, Achieving for Children, Twickenham, London

Practitioners should ask, 'Does this activity support the physical and mental wellbeing of the child and family?' If not, 'Why are we doing this?'

Practitioners need to be prepared to have difficult conversations with parents when alerted to signs of neglect, including untreated medical conditions. Staff meetings are an opportunity for practitioners to discuss how and when to have difficult conversations with parents about issues such as thread worms, head lice, obesity, underweight child, poor oral health, cleanliness, picking children up by the arm, challenging behaviour, etc.

Practitioners can encourage parents to ask for help from health services. For example, a parent explained that their child was dribbling because he had a persistent sore throat. By regularly reviewing and discussing the child's health, the parent was confident to regularly return to the general practitioner (GP – doctor) until the child was referred to a specialist doctor.

Children in the borough have access to development checks at one and two years old but some families miss appointments due to changing address or health service. I observed a child who wasn't eating properly and had tooth decay. To increase his calorie intake the parents gave him milkshakes which were high in sugar. It was a difficult conversation to raise because the family were learning to speak English and the child had complex needs not yet known to a health professional. I advised the parents to register with the dental and health service. The child received dental treatment and accessed specialist support.

Physical activity should be fun, enjoyable and available in all seasons. Many families live in flats or shared accommodation and do not have easy access to outdoor spaces for children to run and make noise. The children's centre provides outdoor play even in colder months; however, some parents complain saying 'it's too cold to play outside', even though the children appear happy and active outside. Practitioners should sensitively inform parents of the benefits of outdoor play and exposure to daylight in winter, the effects of vitamin D deficiency and seasonal affective disorder (SAD) on children, especially when we notice changes in children's behaviour and mood during winter months.

In the crèche, practitioners highlighted issues related to 'separation anxiety'. For example, non-English-speaking parents attending the English class are upset because their toddlers are distressed and crying in the crèche. Practitioners identified that parents and children would be better supported and equipped to cope if offered 'settling-in sessions' prior to starting. We should also simplify our documentation and use visual props such as pictorials, photos and objects to help non-English-speaking parents and children understand how the crèche works and what to expect. To improve the situation, we are going to investigate and share examples of good practice in our team meetings.

Be mindful when simplifying information for non-English-speaking parents that we do not miss opportunities to identify need by not asking about children's eating habits, oral health, sleep, health checks and language development, etc.

Because interpreters are expensive, practitioners sometimes ask English-speaking spouses to interpret on their behalf. I attended a meeting where the parent was a victim of domestic violence. It can be a real issue and concern for victims if their abusers are their main source of information, as their translators, because the abuser receives all the information and may withhold it. In some cases this could also be a breach of trust and victims stop trying to seek help because they have to rely on their abuser for translation. The centre provides free English classes to help parents learn English so that they can communicate independently.

Hygiene and health practices vary among the teams who use the centre, such as the wearing of protective clothing when changing nappies, the cleaning of toys, and hand washing after coughing and sneezing.

An assistant from the Speech and Language Therapy team attends a weekly 'Stay and Play' session. Any parent can discuss their child's language development before it becomes a concern and children who need support are identified early. Parents have reported how they are able to support their child better at home using the advice and strategies demonstrated. In my experience, this is very effective service which families living elsewhere would benefit from if not already available.

Parents tell me that they fear feeling unwelcome or judged by adults because their child has tantrums or hurts others. To support parents, professionals could demonstrate proactive strategies in real-life situations. For example, offer to support the parent whose child is having a tantrum by directing the child who wants to throw objects to a more appropriate activity, thus helping a child to manage a change in the routine. If families isolate themselves, the impact increases the risk of stress, vulnerability and exclusion of developmentally-appropriate experiences and socialisation for the child.

It is our role to help parents feel safe – emotionally and physically – through positive relationships, without shame or blame. We need to recognise when we cause families stress by our words or actions. I have highlighted to colleagues who have criticised a parent's play skills that some parents find play difficult, especially when families are experiencing multiple problems that inhibit wellbeing. However, over time, practitioners can support parents to join in with their child's play through sensitive role modelling.

The children's centre hosts regular multi-agency meetings to facilitate collaborative working between health professionals and early years practitioners. If local nurseries participated they would understand the role of the children's centre and local services. For example, a nursery manager was supporting a family who had a bereavement but had not contacted any other service to access support for the family. This highlighted to me that the role of the children's centre is not fully understood or utilised by local nurseries.

The health visitor (HV) team visit family's homes and identify hidden needs, such as health issues, depression, family breakdown, poverty and neglect. With the family's permission, the HV will ask the centre to invite the family to sessions. The centre can also arrange for the family to be supported in sessions until they become more confident. Without the HV team and other professionals encouraging vulnerable families to attend the centre we would not be able to support them and their situation could worsen. Vulnerable families have reported how much they and their children have benefitted from attending the sessions.

Tom Maybey from Kew, Mortlake, Barnes East Sheen Children's Centres, Achieving for Children, London

Health of toddlers is ingrained into the EYFS through the prime area of physical development. It is easiest to concentrate on the moving and handling aspects through things like exercise and physical exertion, but I have found that the Toddler Wellbeing project has given me more reason to bring elements from health and self-care into practice. Through the recommendations from the toddlers' mealtimes we have encouraged more parents and carers in the 'Stay and Play' sessions to let their children try new and healthy foods, and have put steps in place to make it easier to manage their own hygiene by washing their hands at a child-height sink (or have easy access to other hand-washing facilities). I have also found myself many times telling parents to let their child have a go themselves, with a couple later telling me they then extended their child's independence by letting them wash themselves in the bath at home – it may have been messier and wetter, but it is a step towards improving their child's wellbeing.

SPAIN

Mireia Miralpeix Anglerill and Mª Àngels Domènech Pou from Mas Balmanya Escola Bressol Pública, Surara Serveis, Cataluña

When we talk about wellbeing, we are often talking about physical health, as if it were something that did not concern us at school, at least in terms of physical discomfort or illness in children.

At Mas Balmanya, we have primarily worked on the issue of health from the standpoint of prevention, by fostering healthy habits, creating a pleasant and safe environment and establishing and following hygiene rules for both adults and children. We have also received first-aid training and read documentation on different situations that may arise at school (allergies, intolerances, etc.).

After a careful reading of the ToWe Project manual on wellbeing (Sutherland and Mukadam, 2018) and the debate that it sparked among the teaching staff, we began to question and reconsider the role of physical health in our day-to-day lives and how we deal with it at school:

- What guidelines do we give the families?

- How do we work with the families on the issue of 'ill' children coming to school?

- What documentation do we have?

- How do we have it organised?

- Where in the school is it?

- What protocol do we follow if there are accidents at school?

- What is our relationship with the paediatric service at the Basic Health Centre?

After these initial reflections, we realised that we had to give a more important role to the issue of physical health at school, so we set out to:

- Reconsider how we work with families so that they can respect the instructions and guidelines provided by the school on illness, based on an understanding of their importance with regard to the children's wellbeing instead of merely being an imposition.

- Develop an action protocol in the event of accidents or emergency situations at school: how we should act, who should do what, what processes we should follow, where and how it is written down. When situations of this kind have arisen, we have discussed it with the team and taken different decisions, which we want to record in writing and make part of the school's basic documentation which all new professionals must read.

- Develop a school health folder which organises a wide range of documentation on this topic.

- Contact the paediatric service to agree upon guidelines for health recommendations so the same message is being given by both the primary care facility and the school, reinforcing the importance of the children's physical wellbeing. This communication should make it possible to open up a more direct relationship between the town paediatric service and the school.

- Hold talks for parents on health-related topics.

Conclusion

This chapter has highlighted the importance of understanding how to support toddlers' physical and mental health through a range of strategies including mindfulness, exploring the impact that these have on toddlers' health. The international and national contexts have been identified in relation to supporting toddlers' physical and mental health through UK governmental programmes and initiatives.

Some of the common and rarer childhood illnesses that toddlers may experience have been identified with strategies for EYPTs to use to recognise and be aware of these. Whether a toddler is ill or well they will have a range of needs and abilities and factors that inhibit their wellbeing. This chapter has acknowledged the need for an inclusive and equitable practice that adheres to statutory requirements to help toddlers reach their full potential.

Health checks, immunisation programmes, two-year progress checks and other initiatives used within England have been identified with strategies to support awareness of what they are and how settings can ensure that their responsibilities are being met.

EYPTs' experiences, reflections and strategies were shared from England and Spain. This dimension provides EYPTs with an understanding and awareness of how to support and promote toddlers' health.

The health of a toddler underpins their wellbeing and so interlinks with the other chapters and dimensions.

References

All Party Parliamentary Group on Wellbeing Economics (2014) *Wellbeing in Four Policy Areas.* Accessed 21 November 2017 at http://b.3cdn.net/nefoundation/ccdf9782b6d8700f7c_lcm6i2ed7.pdf

All Party Parliamentary Group on Wellbeing Economics (2015) *Mindful Nation UK: Report by the Mindfulness All-Party Parliamentary Group (MAPPG).* Accessed 21 November 2017 at www.themindfulnessinitiative.org.uk/images/reports/Mindfulness-APPG-Report_Mindful-Nation-UK_Oct2015.pdf

DfE (2017) *Statutory Framework for the Early Years Foundation Stage: Setting the Standards for Learning, Development and Care for Children from Birth to Five.* Accessed 29 January 2018 at https://www.foundationyears.org.uk/files/2017/03/EYFS_STATUTORY_FRAMEWORK_2017.pdf

DoH (2010) *New Horizons: Working Together for Better Mental Health.* Accessed 30 March 2017 at http://toolkit.ineesite.org/toolkit/INEEcms/uploads/1459/UK_Department_of_Health_2010_Confident_communities,_brighter_futures.pdf

DoH and DCSF (2009) *Healthy Child Programme – Pregnancy and the First Five Years of Life.* Accessed 11 March 2017 at https://www.gov.uk/government/uploads/system/uploads/attachment_data/file/167998/Health_Child_Programme.pdf

DoH and DfE (2014) *Special Educational Needs and Disability Code of Practice: 0 to 25 years: Statutory guidance for organisations which work with and support children and young people who have special educational needs or disabilities.* Accessed 20 March 2017 at https://www.gov.uk/government/uploads/system/uploads/attachment_data/file/398815/SEND_Code_of_Practice_January_2015.pdf

DoH and PHE (Public Health England) (2014) *Promoting emotional wellbeing and positive mental health of children and young people.* Accessed 30 March 2017 at https://www.gov.uk/government/uploads/system/uploads/attachment_data/file/299268/Emotional_Health_and_Wellbeing_pathway_Interactive_FINAL.pdf

Kabat-Zinn, J. (2013) *Full Catastrophe Living: How to Cope with Stress, Pain, and Illness using Mindful Meditation.* London: Piatkus.

Marmot, M. (2010) *Strategic Review of Health Inequalities in England Post-2010. Fair Society, Healthy Lives: The Marmot Review Executive Summary.* Accessed 14 March 2017 at www.instituteofhealthequity.org/projects/fair-society-healthy-lives-the-marmot-review

NCB (National Children's Bureau) (2012) *The EYFS progress check at age two.* Accessed 31 March 2017 at www.foundationyears.org.uk/wp-content/uploads/2012/03/A-Know-How-Guide.pdf

NEF (2014) *Wellbeing Economics Report.* Accessed 31 March 2017 at http://b.3cdn.net/nefoundation/ccdf9782b6d8700f7c_lcm6i2ed7.pdf

NHS Choices (2017) *When to have vaccinations.* Accessed 4 April 2017 at www.nhs.uk/Conditions/vaccinations/pages/vaccination-schedule-age-checklist.aspx

NHS England (2016) *Implementing the Five Year Forward View for Mental Health.* Accessed 11 March 2017 at https://www.england.nhs.uk/wp-content/uploads/2016/07/fyfv-mh.pdf

PHA (2013) *Guidance on Infection Control in Schools and Other Childcare Settings.* Accessed 1 August 2017 at www.publichealth.hscni.net/sites/default/files/Guidance_on_infection_control_in%20schools_poster.pdf

PHA (2016) *Nutrition Matters for the Early Years: Guidance for Feeding Under Fives in the Childcare Setting.* Accessed 20 March 2017 at www.publichealth.hscni.net/sites/default/files/Nutrition_Matters_for_the_early_years_LR_06_16.pdf

Public Health England (2014) *Notification of Infectious Diseases (NOIDs)*. Accessed 20 March 2017 at https://www.gov.uk/government/collections/notifications-of-infectious-diseases-noids

Sutherland, H. and Mukadam, Y. (2018) *Toddlers' Wellbeing Manual*. ToWe Project 2015–2018. Accessed 1 December 2017 at www.toddlerswellbeing.eu

The Children's Society (2016) *The Good Child Report 2016*. Accessed 29 March 2017 at https://www.childrenssociety.org.uk/sites/default/files/pcr090_mainreport_web.pdf

UNICEF UK (1989) *A summary of the UN Convention on the Rights of the Child*. Accessed 14 March 2017 at https://353ld710iigr2n4po7k4kgvv-wpengine.netdna-ssl.com/wp-content/uploads/2010/05/UNCRC_summary-1.pdf

WHO (2010) *Global Burden of Disease Study*. Accessed 11 March 2017 at www.who.int/pmnch/media/news/2012/who_burdenofdisease/en

WHO (2014a*) Constitution of WHO: Principles. Basic Documents 48th Edition*. Accessed 11 March 2017 at http://apps.who.int/gb/bd/PDF/bd48/basic-documents-48th-edition-en.pdf#page=1

WHO (2014b) *Mental health: A state of well-being*. Accessed 31 March 2017 at www.who.int/features/factfiles/mental_health/en

CHAPTER 4

SETTING ENVIRONMENTS

Helen Sutherland and Yasmin Mukadam

'Every child has the right to the best possible health. Governments must provide good quality health care, clean water, nutritious food, and a clean environment and education on health and well-being so that children can stay healthy. Richer countries must help poorer countries achieve this.'

(UNICEF UK, 1989)

Introduction

This chapter will investigate the components of a learning environment and how this can be used to support toddlers' wellbeing, learning and development. It will provide early years practitioners and teachers (EYPTs) with an understanding and awareness of their environment providing strategies and opportunities to reflect and improve provision and practice. This will include how the environment can be used to create opportunities for play and learning taking into consideration Health and Safety and risk taking within the learning environment. The term 'environment' will be interchangeably used to refer to both the indoor and outdoor environment. The role of EYPTs will be discussed including practitioner training, experience and qualifications, professionalism and the key person approach.

The learning environment is the space that toddlers use to explore, experiment and develop skills and experiences that will support their learning and development. Space is the physical surroundings in which a range of equipment, furniture and resources are arranged and laid out. The role of the EYPT is to provide a safe and stimulating environment both indoors and outdoors. The environment should provide a range of play opportunities to support toddlers' confidence and skills in all areas of learning and development. A quality learning environment provides a rich, safe and stimulating place where toddlers can develop their curiosity and interest. A quality learning environment takes into consideration:

- An understanding of toddlers' needs and interests with an awareness of how toddlers learn and develop.

- Providing play opportunities and experiences where toddlers can explore with and without adult intervention or engagement.

- Supporting toddlers to manage challenges and appropriate risk taking.

Opportunities for play and learning

Play provides toddlers with the time and space to explore and experiment with their environment, making discoveries whilst engaging with their immediate surroundings. Play provides toddlers with the opportunity to develop their unique interests in a fun and spontaneous way. 'Play is the child's means of living and understanding life' (Isaacs, 2013). Play is therefore important in supporting toddlers' learning, understanding and the development of concepts about their world and environment. A key role of the EYPT is to set up the environment to engage toddlers in various playful learning opportunities and trust that this provides toddlers with the opportunities to develop cognitively (Goouch, 2008).

To enable effective play and learning (see Figure 4.1), EYPTs need to be actively involved in the planning, implementing and reviewing of the environment and the play and learning opportunities taking place. This means regularly using audit tools, such as Sustained Shared Thinking and Emotional Well-being (SSTEW) (Siraj, Kingston and Melhuish, 2015), Infant/Toddler Environment Rating Scale (ITERS) (Harms, Cryer and Clifford, 2006), and the strategies and tools within this chapter, to monitor how the toddlers are using the resources, equipment, materials and space to engage in their play and learning.

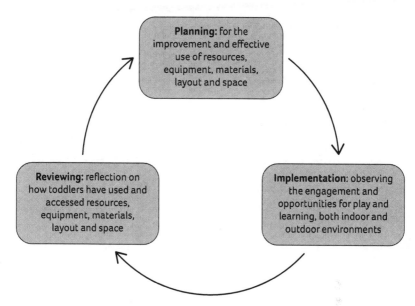

Figure 4.1 – The Play Environment Cycle

Using play as a medium to support learning, it is important to acknowledge the interaction and intervention that play opportunities create (Moyles, 2010). Resources and equipment, such as push and pull toys, places to hide and natural materials and objects provide toddlers with the opportunity to interact and engage with their environment and each other. The play environment should also enable creativity, originality and self-expression both in and outdoors. This can be done through creating stories and narratives, free play activities that encourage spontaneity and including materials and objects that can be explored and manipulated. There are many different educational approaches and philosophies that shape and support this way of working, including the Reggio Emilia approach, Steiner Waldorf approach, Forest School approach and Heuristic play.

Strategies and tools to support opportunities for play and learning

	Evidence	Action
What play opportunities are there for the toddlers in your setting that enable creativity, originality and self-expression, in and out of doors?		
When reviewing the space and environment, how are the following influential in supporting toddlers' opportunities for play and learning: • furniture • layout • access • resources and equipment?		
How often and when are EYPTs interacting and engaging with toddlers in their play?		
What indoor and outdoor activities, resources and experiences are EYPTs providing for toddlers to support needs and interests, exploration, challenges and appropriate risk taking?		

⟳ REFLECTION 4.1

What is your understanding of the role of play to support toddlers' learning within your setting?

Using the planning, implementing and reviewing cycle, review your current environment and identify how the toddlers are using the resources, equipment, materials and space. Reflect and plan how this can be developed and improved to make the most of the play and learning opportunities within the space.

Reflect upon what educational philosophies and approaches are underpinning this.

How can you set up the environment to create a playful experience for toddlers rather than functioning as a space for implementing the curriculum?

What influences how you set up the environment and what is the ideology underpinning this?

Health and safety in the environment

It is the fundamental responsibility of EYPTs to keep children safe, taking into account everyday risks and hazards within the indoor and outdoor environment. This will vary from setting to setting as some practitioners may feel more comfortable with toddlers being involved in risky play than others. There can sometimes be a sense of nervousness where some practitioners may not be confident of toddlers taking risks due to previous experiences. Good management and planning of the environment can help to minimise the risks and hazards while still providing stimulating and challenging play opportunities for toddlers. Risk taking is about EYPTs having the confidence to provide challenging play experiences for toddlers that enable them to take risks, explore and make discoveries about themselves and their environment. This is where good planning can provide opportunities for creative use and managed risk taking in relation to space, layout, resources and equipment both in and outdoors where toddlers can, through the environment, problem solve and develop skills through exploring and experimenting how far they can go and what they can do with the environment and their bodies.

Risk taking can mean different things to different people as what is considered to be a risk for one person may not be for another. This may be due to skills, confidence and experience, for example, one toddler may be confident and experienced in coming down stairs, while another may need to hold a hand for support as they may not have such good balance. EYPTs need to understand each toddler's individual abilities and development to enable challenging opportunities with reasonable risk taking. 'Providers must ensure that they take all reasonable steps to ensure staff and children in their care

are not exposed to risks and must be able to demonstrate how they are managing risks' (DfE, 2017).

The benefits of risky and challenging play are that toddlers can independently develop a range of skills that will support their future learning and development through exploration and experimentation while learning to recognise risks. They can test the environment and their bodies to find out what they can do and practise improving on this. Gill (2007, cited in Knight, 2011) highlighted four arguments in support of risk taking. These included: helping toddlers' natural instinct to take risk through learning to manage risk, understanding the importance of safety in their environment, the benefits of risky play to development and learning, and character building, resilience and perseverance.

An example of how risky play is supported and encouraged in a forest school setting was observed with pre-school children and toddlers playing outside in the stick forest in Sweden. A group of children chose to climb up a 1.5 metre rock that was in the area of the forest that they were in. The children were familiar with this part of the forest. The EYPT observed the children and provided support only when it was needed; if children became unsure or were not confident, the EYPT provided support for children climbing up as to where to put their feet, while other older children also provided help and support. The children then used a tree, very close to the rock, as a firefighter's pole to slide down off the rock. Again the EYPT and older children provided support and encouragement as to where to put feet and how to use the tree to get down.

The Health and Safety Executive (HSE)[1] is the UK national regulatory body responsible for health and safety at work. They provide guidance, advice and examples of how to manage health and safety within the environment, including risk ranking and ratings managing and minimising risk.

Key areas to consider when looking at health and safety within the environment are:

- Legal requirements and regulations, such as risk assessments to identify and minimise hazards.

- Maintaining records and training of staff.

---

1   See http://hse.gov.uk

- Layout, space, access to resources and equipment.

- Adult supervision and facilitation of learning.

- Record keeping and documentation: checklists, risk assessment, incident and accident forms.

- Hygiene and safety of equipment and resources, such as small objects and pieces.

- Medical needs and conditions.

Strategies and tools to support health and safety in the environment

	Evidence	Action
What are your setting's policies and procedures regarding health and safety?		
How is this information conveyed to staff, volunteers, parents, visitors and children?		
What procedures, such as risk assessments and safety checklists, do you carry out and when?		
How do you develop the toddlers' awareness of health and safety within your setting, helping them be aware of risks and hazards during the everyday routine?		

⟳ REFLECTION 4.2

Reflect upon your setting's attitudes to risk taking. How can you support risk taking so that it enhances the toddler's learning experience whilst maintaining and adhering to statutory health and safety requirements?

Learning environment – development and learning

As mentioned earlier, the EYPT plays an integral part in promoting the learning environment through effective planning of the space, layout and resources to establish a flexible and adaptable learning environment. The following areas of learning and development can be used to create a holistic learning experience and link very closely with the next chapter and dimension 4 Toddlers' Development and Learning.

Physical environment

When planning the physical environment it is important to remember the toddler's view, as 'adults admire their environment; they can remember and think about it – but a child absorbs it' (Montessori, 1967, p.57). The EYPT needs to consistently review and ensure a welcoming and attractive environment that encourages a natural curiosity.

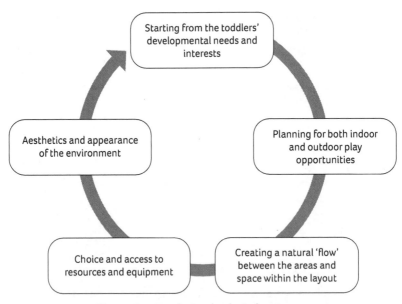

Figure 4.2 – Developing the physical environment

Figure 4.2 demonstrates the key areas for consideration when planning and co-ordinating the physical environment for toddlers to support their continuous wellbeing.

Starting from the toddlers' developmental needs and interests

The needs and interests of toddlers are of paramount importance in creating an interesting and stimulating environment for toddlers that will engage their interests and curiosity. Through observation and discussions with colleagues and families this can addressed as an ongoing bases as toddlers' interests will develop and change.

Planning for both indoor and outdoor play opportunities

Using both the indoor and outdoor environment provides a variety of learning opportunities. The outdoor environment offers a great variation in the climate, weather and seasonal changes that toddlers engage in and notice. The indoor environment can appear to be more structured but this should still offer alternatives and choices that support their interests and stimulate their curiosity.

Creating a natural 'flow' between the areas and space within the layout

This is about creating appropriate space for the natural movement and 'flow' between the different areas of the room. This should enable toddlers opportunities to move unhindered around the room. This should also be between the indoors and out so that toddlers can move freely to choose and experience where their interests are taking them.

Choice and access to resources and equipment

The design and layout of the room is important, taking into consideration how toddlers can access the different resources and equipment provided. It is important not to over stimulate with too many resources and choices so that they may make choices as to what they will access and wish to explore, learning to share and take turns. This will mean providing enough space, opportunities to change what is available and rotating the resources accordingly.

Aesthetics and appearance of the environment

It is important to celebrate toddlers' work and efforts creating displays of their work; however, this needs careful planning to ensure that the setting is not over-stimulating with work, displays and posters, remembering that the environment is what a child absorbs rather than the aesthetic (Montessori, 1967).

Social and emotional environment

Creating a calm, stimulating, safe and friendly learning environment will support toddlers' confidence, wellbeing and self-awareness. Laevers *et al.* (2005) describe that children should feel 'like a fish in water' when they feel alright. The quality of social interactions and communication between staff, the toddler's key person and the toddler is vital in maintaining positive relationships and building self-confidence. Also, being 'in-tune' with the toddler's feelings and emotions, especially when they are engrossed in a learning opportunity, is vital; it is important to give the toddler warnings and choices so they don't feel they are being 'done to'. For example, if a toddler needs a nappy change, are they asked and is their response respected? If this is not the case then invariably they will become distressed and upset at being taken away from the experience without any warning or choice. If their choice is respected invariably they will choose when they are ready to have their nappy changed as it has been bought to their attention.

The role of the EYPT is to provide opportunities, activities and experiences that enable toddlers to express their feelings, such as therapeutic activities like cornflour silk and play dough that can either sooth or calm or release tension and anxieties. This links back to Chapter 3 and dimension 2 with the suggested mindfulness techniques that can be implemented.

Cognitive and language environment

For a successful cognitive and language learning environment the EYPT needs to encourage and facilitate toddlers' exploration, problem solving and development of knowledge through use of positive language and communication. Planning for a variety of exploratory and experiential learning opportunities will engage toddlers' thinking and start toddlers on the route to sustained shared thinking.

EYPTs are responsible for providing a language-rich environment so that toddlers learn to confidently communicate, identify and describe their feelings, ideas, mark making, new words and ways of problem solving.

Strategies and tools to support the learning environment – development and learning

Physical environment	Evidence	Action
What is the physical environment like? Is it welcoming and attractive? What flooring is there to enable different types of activities?		
Assess the appearance of the setting. What is the colour scheme like? Consider the impact of colour.		
What information, posters and displays are there to encourage toddlers' interests?		
How is learning promoted through the different spaces? What opportunities are there in relation to the room layout and structure, access to resources, flow between areas? How is the space being used to promote different learning opportunities?		
What resources and equipment are available and planned for?		
How do they meet the toddlers' developmental needs and interests?		
How does the physical environment encourage both in and outdoor opportunities for toddlers to explore and develop?		

Social environment	Evidence	Action
How do practitioners within your setting model positive behaviour and attitudes?		
How does your setting create an atmosphere where families and toddlers feel welcome and accepted?		
What opportunities does your setting provide for differing types of socialisation to support positive and trusting relationships with adults and their peers?		
How does your setting support and enhance the development of social skills and etiquette, such as sharing and taking turns?		
Emotional environment	Evidence	Action
How does your setting create an inclusive and welcoming environment?		
How do EYPTs support healthy expression of toddlers' feelings and demonstrate that they are listening and tuning in to their voices and non-verbal cues?		
How can EYPTs identify, support and manage toddlers' feelings in a positive way?		
What activities, experiences and events do you provide within the environment that provide toddlers with opportunities to be physically invigorated or soothed and calmed (therapeutic)?		

Cognitive and language environment	Evidence	Action
How does your environment encourage problem solving and exploration to extend toddlers' knowledge and conceptual understanding through the provision of stimulating experiences that draw on their interests?		
How does the setup of your environment encourage toddlers' independent discovery and exploration through the use of resources and equipment?		
How are language and communication skills encouraged and developed for toddlers in your environment?		

⟳ REFLECTION 4.3

Using the following aspects of supporting and promoting the learning environment:

> » The EYPT as a facilitator

> » Spaces

> » Resources

Reflect upon how the physical, emotional, social, cognitive and language environment is supported by each of these aspects.

Staffing

It is important that all staff within the setting adhere to the statutory requirements set out by the government to ensure practice meets all regulatory conditions. Having the right level of staffing is important to make sure that the setting has EYPTs with experience, knowledge and recognised training and qualifications to support the toddlers within their care. Understanding and providing for the wellbeing of staff is a starting point for recognising and nurturing a warm and welcoming environment for all. This includes providing a good working environment and conditions that take into consideration hours worked, equitable roles and responsibilities, support through mentoring and supervision, continuous professional development, career progression, mental health and the health and safety of all staff.

Training and experience

Table 4.1 Levels of qualifications for early years practitioners and teachers

Level	School and university awards	Role in early years
Level 2 (European Qualification Framework – EQF 3)	Introduction to Early Years Education and Care	This level of qualified practitioners will work under supervision and the job roles may include: • nursery or teaching assistant • pre-school assistant • playgroup assistant.
Level 3 (EQF 4)	Early Years Educator (EYE)	This level of qualified practitioners may work in a variety of childcare and educational settings and demonstrate the ability to work independently, supervise and train others and their job roles may include: • day nursery room leader • pre-school leader • childminder • nursery or teaching assistant • community nursery nurse • manager of a day nursery.
Level 4 (EQF 5)	One-year undergraduate degree	Level 4 practitioners may find themselves in management roles in different childcare and educational settings. Their job roles may include: • manager of a day nursery • deputy manager • management responsibilities.
Level 5 (EQF 5)	Two-year undergraduate degree	Foundation Degree award Their job roles may include: (see Level 4)

Level 6 (EQF 6)	Three-year undergraduate degree	Level 6 graduate practitioners demonstrate experience and knowledge across all aspects of early years practice with scope towards leadership and management of provision. Their job roles may include: • manager of a day nursery • deputy manager • management responsibilities • advisor and consultancy roles.
Level 6 (EQF 6)	Postgraduate degree	Early Years Teacher Status (EYTS) and Qualified Teacher Status (QTS) These early years teachers demonstrate an excellence in professional and reflective practice, and their ability to lead and support the practice of others. The skills and experience of early years teachers enable them to lead and inspire colleagues and help give children the start in life they deserve. Early years teachers work in: • day care • schools • pre-school • kindergarten • playgroup.

There are a range of training and qualifications within the sector that allow staff to continually develop their knowledge and understanding as early years educators. Table 4.1 identifies the different recognised levels of qualifications for EYPTs in England.

Your professional role

The professional role of EYPTs includes a range of responsibilities regardless of the country you work in. These may include:

- modelling good practice

- being a reflective practitioner

- leading change and innovation of policies, provision and practice

- encouraging and supporting others in developing their knowledge and understanding
- building positive relationships with toddlers and their families.

(Sutherland and Mukadam, 2018)

The four pedagogical characteristics identified in Chapter 1 underpin the responsibilities of EYPTs in their professional role. Also, when considering the professional role of the EYPT, Brock (2006) identifies key factors that determine the dimensions of professionalism:

- knowledge
- education and training
- skills
- autonomy
- values
- ethics
- reward

(Brock, 2006)

These factors can be clearly reflected in the professional role EYPTs play as they demonstrate a unique expertise in meeting toddlers' needs, good communication skills, sound judgement in decision making, taking responsibility and understanding how to support toddlers' wellbeing (Brock, 2006).

Key person approach

The Early Years Foundation Stages (EYFS) statutory framework for England states that all children must be allocated a key person whose 'role is to help ensure that every child's care is tailored to meet their individual needs to help the child become familiar with the setting, offer a settled relationship for the child and build a relationship with their parents' (DfE, 2017). This legal requirement ensures that there is a universal approach and consistency across early years provision that provides toddlers with a safe and secure environment and person from which they can develop and learn.

This supports and underpins the key theories of John Bowlby and James and Joyce Robertson, of the need that young children have for a secure attachment figure, from which they can explore their environment (Elfer, Goldschmied and Selleck, 2012). This key figure is someone that the toddler has a desire to be near to and seeks out when they need comfort or reassurance. This is about developing an approach that adapts and develops to the toddler's needs rather than being a system that is implemented. This provides young children with a sense of security and belonging which supports play and exploration of new experiences within the setting's environment. It is important that good partnership and communication are built to establish an effective working partnership with parents and to understand the needs of the toddler (Elfer, Goldschmied and Selleck, 2012). The key person approach supports EYPTs to develop a caring, authentic and trusting relationship with each of the toddlers within their key group. This will provide opportunities for the toddler to flourish as they feel safe and secure with their feelings, needs and interests being provided for in a sensitive and caring manner. This also involves supporting toddlers through transitions from settling in to moving on to another setting or room, vertical transitions and transitions within the routine such as nappy changing and snack time and horizontal transitions. As part of the settling-in process the key person needs to be aware of any transitional object that the toddler may be attached to and how to ensure that they have access to this.

The following example shows how the key person approach is viewed through the eyes of children. A group of four three-year-olds is playing at the water tray. When one of them says 'I belong to Linda. Who do you belong to?', another child says 'I belong to Helen'. Each child identifies who their key person is. It is interesting to see from this example how the children demonstrated their view and understanding of the key person approach.

Strategies and tools to support staffing

Staffing	Evidence	Action
How does the setting identify and support the wellbeing of the staff?		
What are the facilities, supervision, continuing professional development opportunities, environment, teamwork, organisation and atmosphere like for the staff working in the setting?		
Practitioner training and experience What current knowledge, understanding or training do staff have that supports their work with toddlers? Identify what future continuous professional development needs the staff in the setting require to fully support the wellbeing of toddlers.		
Your professional role How are Brock's key factors of knowledge, education and training, skills, autonomy, values, ethics and reward reflected within your setting?		
Key person approach How does your setting make provision for the vertical and horizontal transitional processes that toddlers face? How does the key person build and establish caring, authentic and trusting relationships with their key toddlers ensuring that intimate care needs are met by the key person? Does the setting allow for toddlers to change or select their key person? How does the setting respond if this happens?		

↻ REFLECTION 4.4

Professionalism

Applying the four pedagogical characteristics (read and research, critical thinking, reflective practice and skills and attitudes) from Chapter 1, reflect upon how each dimension of professionalism influences you as a professional in your current job role.

Key person approach

» What are the reasons and research underpinning the key person approach?

» How does your setting key person approach policy reflect this?

» How is the key person approach implemented within your setting and how can this be developed further to support toddlers' wellbeing?

Reflect upon how your setting uses the key person approach to support toddlers' sense of belonging.

EYPTs experiences, reflections and strategies from England, Norway and Spain

ENGLAND

Janette Barber from Heathfield Children's Centre, Achieving for Children, Twickenham, London

We used workplace discussions, surveys, audits, filming and displays to reframe our understanding of 'wellbeing', agreeing action plans to make 'wellbeing' visible for practitioners, families and children. Investigating 'wellbeing' brought the team closer, one practitioner said, 'it's an amazing project'.

Voice/sense of belonging

We asked families for feedback, 'I like it here because...my child likes it here because'. We displayed the information and used it to improve practice. One mother said, 'if my children are happy here, I am happy, happy children, happy parent, nothing else matters'.

We are working with parents to capture and celebrate 'Wow! Moments'. Families proudly point out their child's 'Wow! Moment' on display. I observed a 'Wow! Moment' when two children joined hands and danced at tidy-up time. When this happens, adults should be mindful not to interrupt this joyful interaction by making requests such as 'tidy up'.

To encourage the voice of non-English-speaking families, we need to provide more pictorial cues, signs, labels and information in other languages. Non-English-speaking parents tell me they are shy to use their own language but feel proud when they see their language displayed.

Crèche
To support the wellbeing of children attending the crèche we identified the need for a settling-in policy and procedure, simplified communication with parents and more support for children and practitioners. A strategy we use to help build relationships and encourage regular attendance is to loan toys and books.

Role modelling
To draw parents into play we use phrases such as 'let's show mummy' – we are conscious of factors affecting parental engagement, such as depression. Role modelling helps build trusting relationships which facilitates families' engagement with services such as 'Home-Start' and parenting courses.

Video
Finding time to observe children is challenging. Filming enabled us to watch sessions, noting significant observations, such as children being excluded by peers. We were then able to support peer interactions better.

Room layout
Applying the concept 'less is more' we removed some furniture and activities to improve access. Less choice made it easier for children to decide what to play with. More children at an activity encouraged sharing, talking and modelling. We displayed pictorial labels to help children make choices.

Hot spots
We identified activities where children talked, such as role play kitchen and toy garage. We opened up these spaces to avoid overcrowding and positioned a practitioner nearby to support children's talk. Parents asked for advice on how they can help children make friends; I designed a handout with strategies to support children's peer interactions. Parents found the handouts useful but still benefitted from role modelling.

Helping the quiet child

We identified a child who is reluctant to speak. Concerned about his wellbeing and wishing to build a trusting relationship, practitioners continued to talk and play alongside him. One day while playing with dinosaurs and blocks (his choice) he suggested that we make a tunnel for the dinosaurs. My patience was rewarded. The combination of practitioner, resources and enabling environment contributed to this success.

Emotions and feelings

Unless there is risk of injury, I respect parents' feelings and give them the opportunity to manage their child's disruptive behaviour by asking them 'did you see what…did?' I support and empower parents and colleagues to manage children's behaviour by demonstrating strategies such as position yourself between two children who are having a squabble to help them calm down. Parents can access targeted support to manage children's behaviour through parenting courses and 'Home-Start'.

Tidy-up time

We noticed that parents were tidying up and not supervising children, which is risky. I designed a handout requesting parents to work with children to tidy away a few toys, highlighting the learning opportunities.

Praise

One student practitioner naturally responds to children's moods and desires. A visiting teacher gave praise for the strategies she was using. The feedback helped the student make connections between theory and practice and boosted her confidence in her ability. It is important that we praise practitioners' natural abilities and support each other to develop further.

NORWAY

Harrieth Elin Kristiansen Strøm from Sandvedhaugen Barnehage, Sandnes Kommune, Sandnes

When our pre-school wanted to look into dimension 3 in more depth, we decided to place a special focus on familiarisation and attachment, as well as the role of adults, particularly in relation to key persons. In August, September and October, pre-schools are going through a period when they have a lot of new children starting in their various groups. We wanted to look more closely at what we could do to make this process as smooth as possible for both the children and the parents, based not only on what dimension 3 said, but also what the other dimensions said.

In Norway, we have had full pre-school coverage in recent years, which means that virtually every child is eligible for full-day pre-school provision, even the youngest children. The model we have been using for familiarisation until now has a number of weaknesses. The plan is rigid in that there is one plan applicable to all the children, with relatively little scope for individual adaptation. For example, we expected all children and parents to need generally no more than three days of familiarisation at the pre-school setting. We may also have had too little focus on guiding the parents and not asked enough questions about the life of the child before they started pre-school.

In our pre-school culture, about one third of those who work in groups with direct contact with the children are teachers. The rest of the staff either have no qualifications or no professional education related to working with children. This means that an important part of the teacher's tasks as educational leader within the group is aimed at providing the rest of the staff and the parents with professional guidance. Being a role model for the other adults within the group is another vital task in the daily work of the teachers, perhaps even the most important.

Initially, four groups at our pre-school wanted to try out the ToWe Project. The four teachers in the various groups and boards became the ToWe Project group, including myself, and drew up a 'template' for implementing the various dimensions within the groups. We decided to work with one dimension at a time, but we continually focused on wellbeing and how to achieve it.

Each dimension began with the project group discussing the theory and reflecting together. We agreed on the initiative areas we would have within each dimension. This opportunity for us teachers to discuss and familiarise ourselves with the theory and reflect on 'old practice' together was not only useful, but also absolutely essential in order to safeguard the project's theoretical platform. We teachers had a strong focus when implementing and guiding the rest of the staff in the group in the busy daily routine.

We also had a 'kick-off' where all the staff in the four groups were given a joint introduction to the dimension we were about to start working with. We had time to discuss the theory together, provide input and reflect on relevant issues.

It was then time to put the theoretical knowledge into practice within the various groups. The teachers prepared individual plans setting out how this should be achieved within their own group. The parents were given both written and verbal information on what the staff were working on at all times and what impact this would have for their children. We tried to ensure that the entire group always reflected what we were focusing on. We stressed that documentation in the form of both pictures and text would represent the group.

We used the group meetings to reflect on practice and to guide and drive the work forward. However, the key aspect was enabling the staff to become more aware of their own practices within the group in their interactions with individual children and the children as a group. Our most important tasks as teachers were to act as role models and observers, to reflect with the staff and to guide. We have found that all the staff became more aware of their own practices and more reflective from a professional perspective. We have more professional focus.

During the familiarisation process, we were much more focused on what role the behaviour of the adults played as regards wellbeing and security. We have used the 'Circle of Security'[2] and become more aware of how the children 'use' us adults for different things at different times, and that as a result it is important that we adults spend time on the floor with the children and are available to them both physically and psychologically. We have learned some lessons through experience. For example, we have concluded that staff who do not work full-time should not be the key contact/person for the youngest children. It became more difficult for the children to develop a strong and secure attachment to the staff and the familiarisation process took much longer when the practitioner concerned was absent on certain days.

Our experience is that a good, caring familiarisation process focusing on a strong and stable attachment between the child and the key person as well as between the parents and the key person has had a major impact on the wellbeing of the family and the child.

We have spent a lot of time reassuring the parents and guiding them in relation to what they can expect during the familiarisation process, both from their children and from us as early years practitioners. In this context, it was apparent to us that secure parents resulted in more secure children. In the four ToWe Project groups, the parents all stated in the annual user

---

2   See http://circleofsecuritynetwork.org

survey that they were very satisfied with their children's familiarisation period at the pre-school.

SPAIN

Mireia Miralpeix Anglerill and Mª Àngels Domènech Pou from Mas Balmanya Escola Bressol Pública, Surara Serveis, Cataluña

The environment at school has always been a part of our job as teachers, and we have tried to create rich, meaningful, aesthetically pleasing spaces with materials that challenge children which are intentionally distributed around the different spaces created. This has become one of the most highly valued aspects by the educational team itself, the families and other professionals who visit the school. Citing Malaguzzi: 'Space as the third educator'.

By reading the materials on wellbeing, we realised that when we spoke about the environment, we were primarily focusing on the more physical aspects of it, that is, how we organised the spaces, what materials we supplied, in what colours, at what heights, with what intentions in mind. Through reflection, we have started to conceive of the environment beyond just these physical aspects and realise that there is a factor that is extraordinarily important in children's wellbeing which we had never directly dealt with before: the adult's attitude.

Based on this, we considered the environment that we offer children through our attitudes and the way we do things. We started this reflection by individually answering the questions cited in the strategies and tools:

- How does your attitude and behaviour provide a positive model for the children? What do you think a positive model is?

- How do you think you create a friendly, pleasant and welcoming environment for children and their families?

- How do you create opportunities for socialisation to reinforce the development of positive relationships with both adults and with other children?

- What actions do you do that show respect for the children, and what actions show a lack of respect?

The outcome of the different team members' contributions provides us with a series of indicators which would define an environment for development and learning that fosters wellbeing. Based on our joint reflection, we came up with four items where we think we can potentially improve, observe each other and observe where we are both individually and as a team, that is, what model of person and relationships do we show the children. These items are:

- tone of voice

- educators speaking amongst themselves while ignoring the children

- asking permission before taking any action directly towards the children

- being mindful of the times we share with the children.

The first step was to define what each of these points meant so that the entire team would share the same concept. We then created observation grids where for one week we recorded how we act in the different situations that arise with the children on each of these items in our day-to-day work. Based on what was written on these grids, we drew up a document whose content was discussed in team meetings. In these sessions, we debated the attitudes described and which ones could be improved, such as the importance of controlling our tone of voice, respecting children's time and speaking individually to each of them. This work served as the foundation for our continued work on our attitudes with plans for training for the entire team from expert professionals and the drafting of a document that would describe the attitudes a professional working at our school should have.

Conclusion

This chapter has explored how practitioners and early years teachers can support the development of the setting's environment through providing opportunities for play and learning, including risky play, while being aware of the health and safety requirements of their work place. The key person approach plays an important part in providing toddlers with a sense of belonging and wellbeing. Staff wellbeing is important too with knowledge, understanding, training and qualifications playing a role in developing the professionalism and expertise that EYPTs have in providing a safe, stimulating and engaging environment for toddlers to reach their full potential. This chapter underpins the next dimension, development and learning, covered in Chapter 5.

References

Brock, A. (2006) 'Dimensions of early years professionalism: Attitudes versus competences?' *Association for the Professional Development of Early Years Educators (TACTYC)*. Accessed 19 April 2017 at http://tactyc.org.uk/pdfs/Reflection-brock.pdf

DfE (2017) *Statutory Framework for the Early Years Foundation Stage: Setting the Standards for Learning, Development and Care for Children from Birth to Five*. Accessed 29 January 2018 at https://www.foundationyears.org.uk/files/2017/03/EYFS_STATUTORY_FRAMEWORK_2017.pdf

Elfer P., Goldschmied, E. and Selleck, D.Y. (2012) *Key Persons in the Early Years: Building Relationships for Quality Provision in Early Years Settings and Primary Schools*. London: Routledge.

Goouch, K. (2008) 'Understanding playful pedagogies, play narratives and play spaces.' *Early Years 28*, 1, 93–102.

Harms, T., Cryer, D. and Clifford, R. (2006) *Infant/Toddler Environment Rating Scale*. New York: Teachers College Press.

Isaacs, S. (2013) *The Educational Value of the Nursery School*. London: British Association for Early Childhood Education. Accessed 16 May 2017 at https://www.early-education.org.uk/sites/default/files/Anniversary%2090th%20Book_ONLINE.pdf

Knight, S. (2011) *Risk and Adventure in Early Years Outdoor Play: Learning from Forest School*. London: Sage.

Laevers, F. *et al.* (2005) SICS: *Well-being and Involvement in Care. A Process-oriented Self-evaluation Instrument*. Accessed 29 January 2018 at https://www.kindengezin.be/img/sics-ziko-manual.pdf

Montessori, M. (1967) *The Absorbent Mind*. New York: Henry Holt and Company.

Moyles, J. (2010) *The Excellence of Play*. 3rd Edition. Maidenhead: Open University Press.

Siraj, I., Kingston, D. and Melhuish, E. (2015) *Assessing Quality in Early Childhood Education and Care: Sustained Shared Thinking and Emotional Well-being (SSTEW) Scale for 2–5-year-olds Provision*. London: IOE Press.

Sutherland, H. and Mukadam, Y. (2018) *Toddlers' Wellbeing Manual*. ToWe Project 2015–2018. Accessed 1 December 2017 at www.toddlerswellbeing.eu

UNICEF UK (1989) *A summary of the UN Convention on the Rights of the Child*. Accessed 14 March 2017 at https://www.unicef.org.uk/wp-content/uploads/2010/05/UNCRC_summary-1.pdf

CHAPTER 5

DEVELOPMENT AND LEARNING

Helen Sutherland and Yasmin Mukadam

'Every child has the right to life. Governments must do all they can to ensure that children survive and develop to their full potential.'

(UNICEF UK, 1989)

Introduction

This chapter will consider the role of early years practitioners and teachers (EYPTs) in supporting toddlers' development and learning in order to reach their full potential. This will include exploring personal, social, emotional and spiritual development and the interaction, engagement, play, attachment and settling-in of toddlers. This will also make links to Chapter 8 with meal and snack times. It will include cognitive, language and communication, attention, voice and expressions, home language and additional languages, making links to Chapters 6 and 7, as well as covering physical abilities and attitudes and behaviour relating to emotional resilience, regulating feelings and behaviours and conflict resolution.

It is important to remember that, although the areas of development are being addressed individually within this chapter, as EYPTs, the toddlers' learning and development must be considered in a holistic manner as each area impacts and informs the others.

Reflective opportunities will be used to develop understanding and awareness of how to support toddlers' development and learning to enhance their wellbeing. Reflections and experiences from early years practitioners and teachers of how they support the development and learning of toddlers in England and Spain will be provided.

EYPTs play an important role in supporting toddlers' wellbeing, through understanding and facilitating development and learning through play. This incorporates having a current knowledge and understanding of toddlers' developmental milestones and how to effectively support their progress in order for them to achieve their full potential in these formative years. 'Every child deserves the best possible start in life and the support that enables them to fulfil their potential' (DfE, 2017). This includes understanding the value of observations and reflecting on how these inform planning around the toddler's interests and developmental needs. This includes having a good knowledge and understanding of how learning and developmental theories impact, influence and underpin the practice and provision of EYPTs.

It is important to consider the setting environment when looking at toddlers' development and learning. This aspect has been explored in Chapter 4, which identified opportunities for toddlers to explore and experiment within their environment.

Personal, social, emotional development and spiritual learning

Personal, social and emotional development and spiritual learning (PSEDS) are fundamental areas in supporting toddlers wellbeing. The development of each area is important in providing toddlers with the skills and attitudes required to enable them as adults to fully participate in and contribute to society and the local community.

Personal development is about the toddler having the opportunity within the setting to develop their self-awareness, self-confidence and self-esteem, which supports the development of their personality and sense of identity.

Social development is about toddlers learning the social skills of interaction, engagement and building relationships with other people both individually and in group situations. This also includes learning to share, take turns and co-operate with others.

Emotional development is about learning how to express and explore their feelings and manage their emotions in a healthy way. The role of the EYPT is to facilitate this within a safe and supportive play environment, so that toddlers can learn to respond appropriately to these strong feelings and emotions.

EYPTs also need to be aware of the spiritual aspect of a toddler's wellbeing, by working in partnership with families to understand and respect the beliefs and values that families hold and how these may impact upon the toddler. The UN Convention on the Rights of the Child (UNICEF UK, 1989) emphasises that:

> every child has the right to think and believe what they choose and also to practise their religion, as long as they are not stopping other people from enjoying their rights. Governments must respect the rights and responsibilities of parents to guide their child as they grow up.

Interaction, engagement and play

EYPTs can support toddlers' personal, social, emotional and spiritual skills through developing the pedagogy of playful learning (Palaiologou, 2016). This involves providing opportunities for toddlers to interact, engage and play individually and in small groups with both children and adults. This enables toddlers to develop and improve their social, co-operative, emotional and independent skills as they engage with each other, with the EYPTs being positive role models in their effective interaction and engagement with the toddlers. The pointers in Figure 5.1 demonstrate the interdependence and importance in supporting toddlers' playful learning.

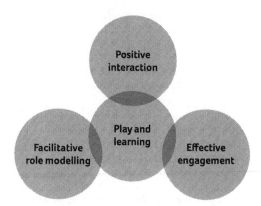

Figure 5.1 – Pointers to support personal, social, emotional and spiritual skills through play and learning

It is important to provide an environment and opportunities for toddlers' self-expression so that they can express their feelings and emotions in a safe and nurturing environment, venting frustrations and learning to cope with their strong feelings. Therapeutic activities such as cooked spaghetti (if the use of food play is allowed in the setting) mixed with paint provides toddlers with a messy, relaxing activity that is open-ended and provides a sensory experience, and enables exploration of the materials and patterns.

This is where the EYPT stands back and observes, providing space for the toddlers' exploration of the material, with support if any toddler is unsure of this sensory experience. EYPTs can at appropriate times provide words to support toddlers with their expressions and feelings, such as, happy, content, brave, brilliant, quiet, calm, settled, relaxed, joyful, fearful, sad, distressed, angry, cross, annoyed, anxious and frustrated. These help toddlers to identify and verbalise their feelings.

The mindfulness activities in Chapter 3 will also help support toddlers' wellbeing, in particular the expression and awareness of their emotional feelings.

Attachment

Attachment is the process by which babies, toddlers and children form a close bond and relationship to their main carer, usually their parent(s), and exhibit distress when they are not in close proximity or are separated from them. The key person approach supports the toddler's need for an attachment figure outside of the home in relation to developing their sense of identity, belonging and security within the setting. The role of the key person is to build positive and trusting relationships with the toddler and their family to understand and meet the needs of the toddler. As mentioned in Chapter 4, the work of Bowlby and the Robertsons have had a key impact upon the need for a key person approach where the key person is attuned to the toddler's individual needs (Elfer, Goldschmied and Selleck, 2012).

Settling-in

Settling-in is commonly known as a vertical transition experienced by most toddlers when they are being introduced to a new experience outside the home. This links closely to attachment and the key person approach, as the key person will become the significant attachment figure within the setting outside the home. The settling-in process provides time for the toddler and parent(s)/main carer to make the transition and form a secondary attachment with their key person. This enables toddlers to build relationships with their key person and to familiarise themselves with the new environment which will then provide them with a sense of identity, belonging and security within the setting.

Meal and snack times

Mealtimes and snack times provide a perfect social opportunity for toddlers to engage in social interaction developing autonomy, independent, personal and social skills. EYPTs are role models in supporting positive examples during these times. Opportunities to cut up their own food using child safe utensils, select their own portion sizes and tidy away afterwards are important skills and experiences for toddlers.

Chapter 8 provides more in-depth understanding of how to support toddlers' wellbeing through mealtimes.

Strategies and tools to support personal, social, emotional and spiritual development and learning

	Evidence	Action
Interaction, engagement and play		
How does your setting make provision to support toddlers' self-esteem, self-confidence and self-awareness through the daily routines and activities?		
What opportunities are provided within your setting to enable toddlers' independence skills and the making of appropriate choices?		
How does your setting support the social skills and opportunities to engage and build relationships and start to build friendships with others?		
How do your setting's policies and procedures enable the healthy expression of feelings and emotions?		

	Evidence	Action
What strategies need further development to support toddlers' healthy expression of their feelings and emotions?		
How does your setting value and respect families' beliefs and values?		
Identify how opportunities for social and emotional aspects of play are evident within the daily routine. For example, cornflour silk provides a therapeutic experience for toddlers.		
How does your setting support toddlers in recognising their achievements, successes and developmental milestones?		
Attachment How does your setting use a key person approach to meet the personal, social, emotional and spiritual needs of the toddler?		
How does your setting sensitively respond, comfort and meet toddlers' emotional needs and behaviours?		
Settling-in What is the settling-in process within your setting and how does it support the toddler and their family during this initial experience?		
What does your setting do to ensure smooth and consistent vertical and horizontal transitions?		
How does your setting use the key person approach to support the settling-in process and toddlers' vertical and horizontal transitions?		
Meal and snack times How does your setting enable toddlers to be independent and autonomous during meal and snack times?		
How are meal and snack times used to develop toddlers' social interaction and engagement with others?		
Use Chapter 8 – Mealtimes audit – to further develop your setting's provision and practice.		

⟳ REFLECTION 5.1

Reflect upon the role of the key person in making provision to support the wellbeing of toddlers.

Take a key toddler that you are concerned about:

» Observe the need or behaviour exhibited by the key toddler.

» Identify strategies, activities and experiences to support the toddler in dealing with and managing their need or behaviour.

» Reflect upon the outcome and success of this intervention.

Cognitive, language and communication development

'Cognitive development is related to thinking and learning skills such as concept formation, problem solving, creativity, imagination, memory, attention and concentration' (Sutherland and Mukadam, 2018). This links to Sustained Shared Thinking (SST) as this approach is about encouraging working together in 'an intellectual way to solve a problem, clarify a concept, evaluate activities, extend a narrative, etc.' (Siraj, Kingston and Melhuish, 2015, p.7). The role of the EYPT is to therefore engage the toddler's thinking in order to facilitate and extend their cognitive learning and development. For this age group the open-ended question of 'what', is more appropriate than 'why', as this better supports their cognitive developmental understanding.

'Language and communication relates to the development of communication skills through speaking (verbal), non-verbal (gesture and body language), listening, reading and writing' (Sutherland and Mukadam, 2018). The EYPT's role is to support, extend and facilitate the language and communication development of toddlers through creating a language rich environment. This includes enabling toddlers to identify and label objects within their surroundings. An example of how toddlers demonstrate this need is through the continuous pointing with the 'what' or 'what's that' questioning to identify and label their environment.

Attention and concentration

Toddlers have a natural curiosity and interest in the world around them and this interest can be used to develop their attention and concentration. Providing a variety of differing learning and development opportunities enables toddlers to explore, experiment and become absorbed within their explorations. The EYPT can facilitate and support the co-construction of toddlers' learning and development through engaging in SST, interaction and collaboration.

Here is an example of how to engage toddlers in SST during storytime. The story of 'The Gingerbread Man' was told to a small group of toddlers through the use of props, which included a tray of grass, a pretend river and all the characters from the story. The toddlers were asked to identify each character as they entered the story, adding them to the tray and identifying the noises they made from a CD recording, creating actions for each animal. The early years teacher then asked: 'How is the Gingerbread Man going to get across the river? What will happen if he gets wet?' After the toddlers' answers, a real gingerbread man was dunked in water and toddlers were asked what has happened to him. The toddlers' reactions were: 'Yuk! Sticky! Wet!' Simple open-ended questions were used to support the toddlers' SST, engagement, social interaction, concentration and language. The story continued with the toddlers' engagement asking what is going to happen next. At the end of the story the toddlers were able to independently retell the story with the resources and props, which they then did for more than 30 minutes.

Voices and expressions

It is important that EYPTs 'tune into' what toddlers are saying verbally and non-verbally through their communication and gesturing. This means listening intuitively to their voice and understanding and respecting what they are conveying in relation to their needs. It is through observation and reflection that toddlers' needs and voices can be heard, understood and made provision for. Being a positive role model is important as developing good language and communication skills enables the healthy expression of feelings and thoughts, as well as developing positive and effective communication skills.

Chapter 6 provides more in-depth understanding of how to support toddlers' wellbeing through supporting toddlers' voices and expressions.

Home language and additional languages

The respecting and valuing of home language(s) is important in providing toddlers with a sense of identity, belonging and security. This ensures that toddlers feel confident in the use of their spoken language, which supports their cognitive development and self-expression. This can be done through learning key phrases in their home language. Mantra Lingua Ltd (2017) provide a range of resources and specific language books for young children, which include talking pens that provide translations to words and story books in 50 different languages.

Chapter 7 will provide a more in-depth understanding of how to support toddlers' wellbeing through supporting their early language(s).

Strategies and tools to support cognitive, language and communication development and learning

	Evidence	Action
Attention and concentration		
How does your setting support toddlers' SST during the daily routines and activities?		
Consider how EYPTs engage in SST to develop toddlers' exploration and creativity of thought through the use of open ended questions such as the use of 'what'?		
How does your setting plan and engage to develop toddlers concentrate during the daily routine?		
What opportunities are being created within the daily routine and activities that take into account toddlers' interests and natural curiosity?		
How does your setting promote learning and development through the use of rhymes, singing, music and stories?		

	Evidence	Action
Voices and expressions How do the EYPTs tune in, listen and respond to the voices, expressions and needs of the toddlers within your setting? How does your setting model, develop and promote the use of positive language? What opportunities are there within the day for toddlers to engage in communication and social interaction with their key person and other children? Use Chapter 6 to further develop your setting's provision and practice.		
Home language and additional languages How does the setting currently recognise and promote toddlers' home language(s)? How can your setting further develop approaches to promote home language(s) through resources, activities, singing, and routines? Use Chapter 7 to further develop your setting's provision and practice		

♲ REFLECTION 5.2

Reflect upon the range of activities, games and experiences that you currently provide for toddlers within your setting and how they encourage concentration, attention, SST and problem solving.

» From this how can these (concentration, attention, SST and problem solving) be further developed and what other effective strategies, activities, games and experiences can be used to promote toddlers' concentration, attention, SST and problem solving?

Choose one of the toddler's favourite stories:

» Break down the content of the story into manageable sections with open-ended questions that can be used to develop SST.

» Identify what resources and props could be used to enhance the story and engage the toddler's interest further.

» Implement the story, observe and reflect upon the toddler's development and learning.

Physical development

EYPTs need to provide indoor and outdoor opportunities for toddlers to practise, challenge and improve their physical abilities and attitudes. These include acquiring the skills and abilities for: balance, co-ordination, spatial awareness, gross and fine motor skills, independence and confidence to move and handle themselves whilst exploring the movement of their bodies and the world around them. A range of activities, experiences and events provide important opportunities for toddlers to practise these skills.

Physical abilities and attitudes

Encouraging and challenging toddlers to have confidence in their physical abilities and to master these physical skills will provide a good foundation for future physical activities. This will help to develop positive attitudes and confidence in trying out new experiences such as sports and other activities as they mature. An example to support this is a toddler learning to climb large play equipment. It is the role of the EYPT to encourage the toddler to independently attempt the steps, which will develop their physical muscle strength, encouraging them to manage the risk for themselves without the need to 'hold' or 'help' them unless there is a safety risk or the toddler is in difficulty. The EYPT needs to be observant of how the toddler is doing, be aware of their physical abilities and development and know when to intervene or to allow toddlers to take risks within a safe environment.

Strategies and tools to support physical development and learning

	Evidence	Action
Physical abilities and attitudes How does your setting provide opportunities for toddlers to develop their physical abilities and attitudes both in and out of doors?		
How does your setting enable toddlers opportunities to develop confidence with their movement and spatial awareness and learn to use their bodies imaginatively?		
How does your setting challenge, encourage and enable toddlers to develop positive attitudes to physical experiences?		

⟳ REFLECTION 5.3

Reflect upon how you challenge and encourage one of your key toddler's development and learning of physical attributes and attitudes:

» Gross motor development

» Fine motor and manipulative skills

» Movement and balance

» Spatial awareness and co-ordination

» Independence, confidence and risk taking

Plan and implement an activity, experience or event for each of the above physical abilities and attitudes that will enable the key toddler to practise, challenge and improve their development.

Behaviour

Behaviour is about how toddlers act and react to experiences and others within the environment around them. The role of the EYPT is to support and enable the healthy expression and strong feelings and emotions that toddlers display, and help them to manage these and to recognise the impact this has upon themselves and others around them.

The main causes of behaviour issues with toddlers are often linked to frustration, asserting their independence, inability to express their feelings and views and lack of resources, which cause issues with sharing and taking turns. This is where the EYPT can support the toddler by ensuring that there are sufficient resources and space that engage the toddlers, facilitating with problem solving, negotiating and decision making, thus enabling opportunities for sharing and taking turns without waiting too long. The adult can support toddlers' expression of feelings and views through a range of planned therapeutic activities. Another way is to provide a range of key words that can help them understand their feelings and help them to express their views so that they feel listened to and do not become frustrated. Offering minimal choices, a selection of two options can enable the toddler to have some control and independence over the situation. Consider the example in Chapter 4 of the nappy changing situation and the difference observed in behaviour where the toddler is given a choice about having their nappy changed.

Emotional resilience, regulating feelings and conflict resolution

'Emotional resilience is the ability to which a toddler learns to manage their feelings and emotions when experiencing stressful or frustrating situations' (Sutherland and Mukadam, 2018). The EYPT plays an important part in supporting toddlers to build their emotional resilience, by providing opportunities to recognise their feelings and outlets for the healthy expression of these emotions and feelings. Also create opportunities for self-expression, self-awareness and understanding of how to deal and cope with these feelings and emotions. This links back to Chapter 3 and the importance of the mindfulness strategies that support toddlers in noticing, describing and expressing their feelings and emotions.

Through the regulation of emotions and feelings, toddlers are able to fully engage and participate in their own learning and development; this supports their overall physical and mental health and wellbeing. Conflicts may still arise with toddlers as they learn to manage social situations therefore EYPTs need to always remain calm within a toddler's emotional situation. They need to recognise and respond to the fact that toddlers may be experiencing heightened emotions and feelings, then discover what has happened, reflecting this back using simple words about what has happened so that the toddler can understand what the issue is. EYPTs can therefore offer toddlers an opportunity to find a solution, providing choices if required and support in resolving the conflict (HighScope, 2016).

Here is an example of applying this strategy. Two toddlers are playing outdoors when one of the toddlers goes over and pushes the toddler playing on the 'play 'n' ride' toy off. This causes the other toddler to cry and scream. The EYPT approaches the toddlers and states that she can see that they are both upset. She comforts and checks that the pushed toddler is okay. The EYPT then talks to both of the toddlers about what has happened, acknowledging their feelings using simple words to identify frustrations. She reminds the toddlers about sharing and being kind. The toddler who has pushed the other toddler is supported in recognising their unwanted behaviour, reminded how to make amends and supported with how to approach and ask for what they would like, using their words rather than unwanted actions.

Strategies and tools to support behaviour

	Evidence	Action
Emotional resilience, regulating feelings and conflict resolution How does your setting provide opportunities to support toddlers in understanding, managing, regulating and expressing their feelings and emotions?		
What experiences, activities and events does your setting provide to support and enable toddlers to be self-expressive?		
How does your setting help toddlers understand, recognise and express their feelings?		
How does your setting support and regulate toddlers' strong feelings and behaviours?		
How does your setting help and encourage toddlers to problem solve and resolve their conflicts?		

⚙ REFLECTION 5.4

Reflect upon a recent conflict that occurred with the toddlers in your setting:

- » What triggered the conflict?

- » How was this addressed and dealt with? What words and actions were used?

- » How were toddlers' feelings and emotions acknowledged?

- » How were the toddlers supported in reaching a resolution?

- » What could have been done differently and how could you further support the emotional resilience of toddlers in your setting?

EYPTs' experiences, reflections and strategies from England and Spain

ENGLAND

Kathryn Hogarth from Kew, Mortlake, Barnes East Sheen Children's Centres, Achieving for Children, London

When working alongside a family to think about their child's wellbeing, it can be so useful to have a document, an audit or a tool to help delve a little deeper into their world. It can also feel quite daunting and intrusive, so it is all about finding the right balance. You need families to feel supported and encouraged by the work you're doing together, not judged or imposed upon.

Once you have built up a good relationship with a family, the audit tool is a good way of asking the more sensitive questions, especially around a family's home situation. As well as understanding the physical structure of the family's home, it is also important to gain knowledge of the parent's ability to provide a clean, warm space and nutritious meals. A setting needs to be aware of how families can access local food banks, fuel grants, support in training or going back to work and support improving daily routines. How can you help? Can the setting provide a hot meal? Are there clothes and toys that have been donated that can be passed on? The family may not be able to move out of an area with a high crime rate, so it's important to know if they can keep the children safe from harm, and if they have a plan of what to do in an emergency situation.

The audit is also a very useful tool to do some self-reflection and think about the opportunities available for the children while they are in the setting. When we looked into the different languages that are spoken in our setting, we were amazed to find it was more than 50. The challenge then becomes how to make this meaningful for the children – it is about moving past having a welcome poster with lots of languages to spending time with the children, looking at books in their language, labelling their favourite toys in their language, having pictures of cultural events and families celebrating together displayed so children can see them and talk about them with practitioners and friends.

You may have the physical environment set so the children have the greatest access and enjoyment, but it is also vitally important to think of how the practitioners are interacting with the children to promote their wellbeing. It is easy to rush over to help, giving a boost to a child trying to climb onto a chair, or cutting out the shape they want with the scissors, but why don't we pause a few seconds? Wait. Watch. Children are often capable of much more than we give them credit for. It might just be that they have never have had the chance to have a go for themselves. It is our responsibility to let them try. We need to set up achievable tasks that when successfully carried out bring the child a wonderful sense of accomplishment.

By providing opportunities to show the children what they can achieve, they are more likely to attempt more activities and have the self-confidence and self-belief to try more things. This is incredibly beneficial for their learning and development, and if you can also show parents these benefits, the children will get more of these opportunities both in the setting and at home.

SPAIN

Natàlia Turmo and Sílvia Turmo from Petita Escola, Barcelona, Cataluña

When starting the project, we wanted to get the families involved from the very beginning. One of the first things we did at meeting with parents was to brainstorm the concept of wellbeing. What does your child's wellbeing mean to you? What has to be done so your child is well at school?

Among many concepts discussed, learning, development, opportunities to learn, a stimulating environment and discoveries were mentioned repeatedly. The school is a space where children develop and learn.

At Petita Escola, the entire team of teachers is aware that children are in the foreground of their own learning. As professionals, our role is to serve as guides, observers, preparers of places and materials; we must know the children and their potential weaknesses. Teachers must serve as role models for the children; we must be energetic while also advocating peace and order, seeking the calmness and safety needed so children develop a desire to investigate and learn.

Around this essential core, the child, is an environment which must be stimulating and rich, an environment which should also educate them, along with professionals who have to be aware of their role as mentors and facilitators of development, who have to be mindful of attitudes, words and subtleties to convey to the children the environment of wellbeing needed so each of them can learn.

The ToWe Project has allowed us to take our reflection to a much deeper level and work on these two aspects: creating stimulating learning environments both indoors and outdoors, and working (both individually/internally and as a group) on the role of the teacher within the group and our attitudes towards the children any time they are at school.

Regarding the spaces, we have organised the classrooms in such a way that the children are always in different play areas (make-believe with dolls and a kitchen; a construction zone with ramps, cars and trains; an art zone with an easel and a cart with materials to design, shape, paint; an experimentation table with natural materials to play with, like sand; a story corner; a zone with musical instruments and puppets). Since the nursery school was created, we have been mindful of the importance of having high-quality materials (natural, crafted of wood, carefully chosen stories, rich illustrations that the children enjoy and learn from seeing; materials created in-house, etc.). Based on the training and exchange from the ToWe Project, we have also tried to present the materials in a way that is both attractive and stimulating for the children by setting up the shelves in such a way that there are fewer resources and they are all within the children's reach. Giving them the freedom to choose what they want to use when was the key to lowering the level of conflicts in the classroom and enjoying a rich, quiet play environment. If play is the main source of learning, then children must be given opportunities to play with a wide variety of toys targeted at their different objectives, interests and concerns. Here the teacher's capacity for adaptation or flexibility also comes into play when adapting the resources and spaces to the different groups, children or times in the academic year.

In the outdoors areas, gardens, terraces or playgrounds, we have followed the same process, transforming flat, grey areas overly focused on the children's motor development into greener, warmer spaces with a variety of play resources: structures for climbing up and down or hiding; spaces where the children can play with sand; make-believe play areas like a kitchen or a supermarket; and mural panels to stimulate and play with the senses of touch, hearing and sight. The activities we offer the children every day are meant to stimulate them as they have fun. They range from motor activities to musical, artistic, literary, experimental or manual activities. The psychomotor and musical activities are led by experts in psychomotor development and music, who are familiar with the children from when they start school at the age of four months and continue with them until they are three years old. The other activities are presented by the other teachers, always in pairs: one speaking in Catalan (the native language of the vast majority of the children at the school) and one speaking in English (which we introduce as an additional language). While until relatively recently, the open play time was stopped to start an activity, now, after reflecting on children's learning and development and wellbeing, participation in the activity has become optional. In this way, the children come to participate in those activities in which they are truly interested, while those who are motivated by exploring, playing or discovering in another learning zone are free to do so. Respect for each child's desire to learn must come before the teachers' desire to teach. However, we are pleased that the activities are usually met with excitement and high expectations by the entire group, a signal that they suit their interests, tastes and abilities. The change in pace created by these brief moments helps the children learn a dynamic and routine that gives them peace of mind and security, one that facilitates their autonomy and helps them move towards the next step. It also allows us to work with them on the pleasures of silence, attentiveness, active listening, observation and knowledge of the rest of the group. We are already working to even further enrich these activities to turn them into true moments of enjoyment and learning.

Conclusion

This chapter has identified some of the areas and aspects that are important in supporting toddlers' development and learning to reach their full potential. Links have been made to Chapters 6, 7 and 8 and how they can be used to support toddlers' voices and expression, early language(s) and mealtime. It has provided examples of practice to support toddlers' development and learning in exploring personal, social, emotional and spiritual, interaction, engagement and play, attachment and settling-in, highlighting how SST can be used to support cognitive development through the use of open-ended questions. The importance of creating a positive and language-rich environment to support toddlers' language and communication skills has been discussed. The physical skills required to support toddlers' development of abilities and attitudes has been explored with an example to emphasise enabling independence and risk taking. The chapter has concluded with the importance of recognising and supporting toddlers in understanding and managing their feelings and emotions to support emotional resilience, regulation of behaviour and conflict resolution.

References

DfE (2017) *Statutory Framework for the Early Years Foundation Stage: Setting the Standards for Learning, Development and Care for Children from Birth to Five.* Accessed 29 January 2018 at https://www.foundationyears.org.uk/files/2017/03/EYFS_STATUTORY_FRAMEWORK_2017.pdf

Elfer, P., Goldschmeid, E. and Selleck, D. (2012) *Key Persons in the Early Years: Building Relationships for Quality Provision in Early Years Settings and Primary Schools.* 2nd Edition. London: Routledge.

HighScope (2016) *Social Development: Learning to Resolve Conflicts.* Accessed 1 February 2016 at https://highscope.org/curriculum/preschool/details

Mantra Lingua Ltd. (2017) *Mantra Lingua.* Accessed 24 July 2017 at http://uk.mantralingua.com

Palaiologou, I. (2016) *The Early Years Foundation Stage: Theory and Practice.* 3rd Edition. London: Sage.

Siraj I., Kingston D. and Melhuish E. (2015) *Assessing Quality in Early Childhood Education and Care: Sustained Shared Thinking and Emotional Wellbeing (SSTEW) Scale for 2–5-year-olds Provision.* London: IOE Press.

Sutherland, H. and Mukadam, Y. (2018) *Toddlers' Wellbeing Manual.* ToWe Project 2015–2018. Accessed 1 December 2017 at www.toddlerswellbeing.eu

UNICEF UK (1989) *A summary of the UN Convention on the Rights of the Child.* Accessed 1 February 2016 at https://www.unicef.org.uk/wp-content/uploads/2010/05/UNCRC_summary-1.pdf

CHAPTER 6

EXPRESSIONS IN PLAY

Yngve Rosell and Monika Röthle

'Every child has the right to express their views, feelings and wishes in all matters affecting them, and to have their views considered and taken seriously. This right applies at all times, for example, during immigration proceedings, housing decisions or the child's day-to-day home life.'

(UNICEF UK, 1989)

Introduction

In this chapter we will present perspectives and views about the adult's role and toddlers' play in early years settings. Our aim is to offer political, theoretical and empirical views and knowledge that can be used to reflect upon practice and to discuss how to support toddlers' expressions in play. We will give a description of the UN Convention on the Rights of the Child, changes and research on the views of toddlers, as a foundation to reflect upon the adult role in supporting toddlers' expressions. The theoretical framework for this chapter is based on Merleau-Ponty's (2002) description of the 'Lived-Body' where the body and bodily expressions are the starting point for the body–subject's intertwined interactions with other body–subjects and the world. The theoretical understanding of interaction is also supplied with Skjervheim (2001) and Løgstrup's (2010) description of 'a third party'. Some of the aspects of this theoretical framework are used as a base of knowledge and exemplified through Nordic interpretive qualitative research. Some of the main findings from the presented empirical research are further organised as reflective guidelines and questions that can be used in discussions in team settings. In conclusion we sum up and present some experiences from practitioners that have used these reflective guidelines and questions in the ToWe Project.

The UN Convention on the Rights of the Child – the child's right and the early years practitioner's and teacher's role

The United Nations Convention on the Rights of the child (UNCRC) (UN General Assembly, 1989) states that all human beings – regardless of age, gender, race and ability – shall be treated with respect and dignity on their own premises. The implementation of this Convention, signed by many countries, is a great challenge to politicians, lawmakers and other stakeholders in society. For practitioners in early childhood education the question is: what does it mean to treat children with respect and dignity on their own premises? Rights and duties are interconnected concepts; the accomplishment of rights depends on someone's responsibility to ensure the rights. In the context of early years settings, this is about the role and responsibility of the early years practitioner or teacher (EYPT).

Two documents of the UNCRC offer some explanations of what this might imply: 'Implementing child rights in early childhood' (UNCRC, 2005) and 'The right of the child to be heard' (UNCRC, 2009). They emphasise that implementing children's rights means rethinking the EYPT's role in early childhood:

> A shift away from traditional beliefs that regard early childhood mainly as a period for the socialization of the immature human being towards mature adult status is required. The Convention requires that children, including the very youngest children, be respected as person in their own right. (UNCRC, 2005)

This is a radical interpretation, as they argue that there is no limitation to age. Even the newborn is entitled to the dignity of a person. The request is to perceive the young child as a complete person and to think less of overcoming their immaturity. However, is it reasonable to disregard the differences in maturity?

Let us look to Article 12 of the UN Convention, stating that the views of the child have to be given due weight in 'accordance with the age and maturity of the child'. Here the convention talks about 'according to their maturity' (UNCRC, 2009). This phrase relates to the overall issue of the Convention: the child's right to protection. Toddlers are vulnerable and not expected to be mature enough to take responsibility for themselves. Therefore, it is the society's duty to ensure the protection of the child and its family. However, can infants and toddlers express their views? The document claims that children are able to 'make choices and communicate their feelings, ideas, and wishes in numerous ways, long before they are able to communicate through the conventions of spoken or written language' (UNCRC, 2005). Thus, the document states that toddlers can express their view in many kinds of 'languages'. We have to look for more than words when it comes to toddlers' voices. The document continues: 'Consequently, full implementation of Article 12 requires recognition of, and respect for, non-verbal forms of communication including play, body language, facial expressions, and drawing and painting, through which very young children demonstrate understanding, choices and preferences' (UNCRC, 2009). This means adults have to be aware of what children express through play, facial expressions, gaze, gestures and the whole body. Furthermore, adults have to respect these utterances as adequate and meaningful forms of communication.

♻ REFLECTION 6.1

Think of episodes of communication with an infant.

    » What did the infant express and by which means?

    » How could you be able to interpret the infant's 'message'?

    » Are you sure you got the message right?

    » Is it possible to avoid misunderstanding? If yes, how? If not, why?

The fulfillment of the child's rights depends on the adult's responsiveness to the child's expressions. The UN document outlines the desired quality of the adult's interaction with the child like this:

To achieve the right of participation requires adults to adopt a child-centered attitude, listening to young children and respecting their dignity and their individual points of view. It also requires adults to show patience and creativity by adapting their expectations to a young child interests, levels of understanding and preferred ways of communicating. (UNCRC, 2005)

The quote uses many positive words to describe the requested adult attitudes and acts: listening, using creativity, being patient and child-centered, in order to adapt to the child's interest and conditions. It is easy to agree to such ideals, but much more difficult to live them in everyday practice.

Berit Bae, a Norwegian researcher, has identified some problematic issues in the way Norwegian early childhood education and care (ECEC) settings have responded to the UN Convention (Bae, 2010). It seems like the child's right to participation is interpreted with a bias towards individualism, meaning too much effort is put on the individual child's freedom of choice and less on the child expressing their views together with peers. Bae also asks for a deeper understanding of the importance of play in relation to the child's right of freedom of expression. When researchers asked children what they prefer to do in their setting, the majority of the children answered 'play or to be with friends' (Søbstad, 2004, cited in Bae, 2010). They also told that they play to have fun and for the sake of playing. Based on the children's clear answers, Bae suggests play and playful interaction as children's preferred mode of expression (Bae, 2010). In playful interactions with adults and peers, children can exercise their right to participation and freedom of expression. However, this depends on what EYPTs regard as appropriate ways of playing and how they structure playtime and the daily routines.

Summary

The implementation of the UN Convention in early years settings is a demanding, continuous journey. There are no simple methods of how to make this work, but we can attempt to give more space for the child's right to influence than we did before. Often children express that their preferred mode of expression is play. Therefore, we will invite you to observe and elaborate toddler's interactions in play. As outlined above, the realisation of children's right requires a rethinking of the child as a person as well as the role of the early childhood practitioner. We will therefore challenge you to reflect on your assumptions about toddlers and what you might take for granted.

♻ REFLECTION 6.2

What do you mean by 'respecting the child's dignity'?

In which situation do you think EYPTs might possibly offend the young child's dignity?

Psychology's changed view of the toddler

Developmental psychology deals with how children gradually build up their motor, social, moral, linguistic and cognitive skills until they reach the adult state. The early theories (such as Jean Piaget) outlined children's limitations in relation to their understanding of the concept of time, relative inability to predict the consequences of their actions and relative inability to regulate their emotions. These theories do not claim that toddlers are worth less than adults are, rather that toddlers act on different premises than adults. According to John Bowlby (1969), the child is vulnerable and in need of protection, closeness and maternal care in order to develop a healthy personality.

In line with improved research methods, psychologists emphasise the infant's competences. Researchers have recently been describing infants as able to look for objectives and meaning in their world, from birth onwards (e.g. Gopnik, Meltzoff and Kuhl, 1999). A dominant model of understanding in modern developmental psychology is the transactional model, in which the focus is on how the characteristics of the toddler and the characteristics of the environment continually influence and affect each other over time (Sameroff, 1987). We cannot explain the development of a toddler solely by the influence of the environment on the toddler, since the characteristics of the toddler, such as temperament, also influence how the caregiver socialises with the toddler, which in turn is affected by how the adult interprets the toddler's behaviour. This means that different toddlers will provoke different reactions from the same environment.

However, the same toddler will also react differently within different environments. The transactional model claims that the toddler and the environment are shaped by one another. Daniel Stern (1985), who has played an extremely significant role in developing the adult understanding of children as competent, has shown the significance of the mutual relationship between caregivers and the infant's innate ability to interact. Several researchers highlight the interaction between a toddler's abilities and its environment, and how these interactional experiences contribute to the toddler's steadily increasing understanding of itself, other people and the world. They draw attention to the manner in which the toddler's individual development always takes place in the context of relationships and interaction. Sommer (2014) uses the term 'relative resilience' to show that the toddler is both competent and vulnerable.

A theoretical framework for toddlers' expressions – the lived body

This chapter's theoretical framework for understanding toddlers' expressions in play, their expressions in many kinds of 'languages' (e.g.UN Convention) and their interaction with the environment, is based on the French philosopher Maurice Merleau-Ponty's (2002) description of the body as a form of expression. Merleau-Ponty is not concerned with the body as a tool or with the toddler's motor skills, but with the fact that the body forms the basis for the toddler's perceptions of the world. The body is a part of our existence, our base/starting point for being in the world, and it is through the body that the toddler experiences the world. The body holds experiences, skills, opinions and wishes, long before we can express them with words. Bodily expressions represent both what is observable and the toddler's inner emotional life. Merleau-Ponty's theory gives assumptions of the world's ambiguity and complexity. He uses the concept 'lived body' to describe that the body is both individual and social, inner and utter, subjective and objective. The lived body has a past, a present and a future. The body is situated in a social world; perceiving and experiencing in a world consisting of other lived bodies. Children understand relationships with adults and their peers, with things and activities, through the body. It is in this kind of interaction that children can form new experiences and develop their understanding of themselves and the world. A prerequisite of this is that the content of the toddler's expressions must be recognised, that is that we facilitate or support the experiences, skills, opinions and wishes that the toddler presents through its expressions.

The theory that the body is the basis for toddlers' understanding of themselves, other people and the world they live in, is also a theory that challenges the idea about what content should be attached to various 'phenomena' in the early years setting. According to Merleau-Ponty's (2002) theory, we perceive things in the world as 'phenomena' (e.g. toys and furniture as tables, chairs, closets, etc.). A phenomenon is: 'something that appears, for someone, a subject' (Bengtsson, 2005). An expressed meaning considering a phenomenon is grounded in the body and the bodily experience – which means that both toddlers and adults can have different views and understanding of a phenomenon.

Based on Merleau-Ponty (2002), communication and expressions can be described as gestures, facial expressions, emotional expressions, sounds, words and body position (Rosell, 2016). In relationships with other people, the emotional aspects of the bodily expressions (the 'lived body') are also a central part of safeguarding toddlers' behaviour. Stern (1985) refers to the term 'affective attunement' as an example. This term describes that when a toddler encounters a caregiver, the caregiver feels, experiences and recognises the toddler's own feelings behind an expression. Moreover, the toddler experiences that the caregiver returns those feelings in an interaction – not just a simple imitation of that expression (for example, a toddler crying because they miss their mother or father, or crying after a conflict with peers). Safeguarding the toddler's emotional expression, and not least safeguarding the toddler's emotional development/development of the self (Stern 1985), thereby becomes important in order to support and safeguard children's expressions and their rights – just as these are also stipulated in the United Nations Convention on the Rights of the Child.

Previous research indicates that taking the initiative, opening up to others – a kind of reciprocity – are important in relationships both with peers and adults (Burleson, Delia and Applegate, 1992; Corsaro, 1997; Engdahl, 2011; Greve, 2007; Hazen and Black, 1989; Løkken, 2000; Michélsen, 2004). Rosell (2016) describes that being a guide, having a guiding function by being the one who takes initiative and comes up with ideas, can also be important when toddlers form an understanding of themselves and the world. Someone has to take an initiative and create a relationship and a common world that exists for both (Merleau-Ponty, 2002). Maintaining toddlers as subjects in relationships both with peers and adults can be related to the

Norwegian philosopher Hans Skjervheim's (2001) description of an encounter with a mutual 'third'. Skjervheim (2001) writes that an encounter between two subjects comprises more than a mere meeting between two people, it is an encounter in which two subjects are sharing something; which he describes as 'the third' of a common focus and commitment. Løgstrup (2010) describes that 'the third' in an encounter consists of activity and/or personal aspects. Encounters between human beings are around something: 'a third party' which we share, focus on, quarrel about or enjoy together. In the context of an early years setting, examples of this 'third' could be the common understanding and commitment to a toddler's experience, the toddler's initiative, a book, a song, toys, an activity, emotional expressions, and so on. In toddlers' shared play, this common ground could be based on personal aspects (e.g. friendships) and/or through a variety of activities (e.g. play routines, construction play, negotiations and conflicts). Supporting toddlers' initiatives and toddlers' play, through reciprocity or being a guide and maintaining a common focus and commitment, is an important role for the EYPT. It is by sharing the toddler's experience, their expressions and their initiatives with objects (understood in a phenomenological sense – as phenomenon) that the adult can confirm and recognise the toddler as a subject of its own, a human being, and develop what toddlers express as meaningful in play.

Adults' views on toddlers

Fostering children's development is a main mission of early childhood education. EYPTs hold different views on children. The manner in which we define toddlers is significant to the way in which we socialise with them and the care we give them. Our view of the toddler is related to how we as adults 'perceive, interact with and relate to' toddlers as people (Johansson, 2013). It can be difficult to express our own perceptions of toddlers as people, but the way different adults socialise with toddlers in the setting tells us something about their views of the toddler. Swedish researchers studied the interaction between adults and toddlers at 30 early years centres, and found that the staff mediated three different views, which are presented through the following headings (Johansson, 2013). Under the heading 'adults know best', the EYPTs are described as acting primarily on the basis of their own perception of what is best for the toddler. EYPTs who think that toddlers are irrational are presented under the heading 'toddlers are irrational', while those who think that toddlers also have intentions and interests which should be respected are presented under the heading 'toddlers are human beings' (Johansson, 2013). Let us take a closer look at what these three different perspectives involve.

Adults know best

What characterises this mode of relating to toddlers is the fact that the adults act on the basis of their own view of what is best for the toddler. The EYPTs believe that it is their goal to do what is best, and therefore do not find it necessary to relate to the toddler's way of looking at things. As a result, the asymmetry between the toddler and the adults becomes entrenched, and the toddler becomes an object in the adults' efforts to achieve their goal. EYPTs may well give the 'toddler a right to choose, but the choice is based on the adults' structure' (Johansson, 2013). An example of this is when a toddler is apparently given a choice, such as whether or not they would like more apples, but with the adult passing over the piece of apple without waiting to hear whether the toddler says yes or no. The toddler does not participate in the decision. In situations where toddlers and adults have different wishes, the EYPTs may also first go along with a toddler's wish, for example to wear a particular hat, only then to swap the hat for another one without the toddler's knowledge. What the toddler expresses has little significance, because it is the 'adults who know what is best for the toddler'. Toddlers do not know what is best for them, and therefore have to submit to the adults' will. They must learn to cope with adversity and follow rules. For example, all toddlers should eat all of their food. The consequence of such a rule can be that toddlers are forced to eat food, although the adults may also feel that using their position of power is unpleasant. In such situations, EYPTs have to step back from their emotions, in order to ignore the toddler's reluctance. The argument that 'only adults know best what is best for the toddler' can then be used to justify this lack of empathy with what the toddler is feeling.

Toddlers are irrational

The assumption that toddlers act without the ability to learn from their experiences and create meaning often arises in situations in which a toddler does something they are not allowed to do. In such situations, there is a tendency for adults to think that the toddler has acted without a real purpose, or that the purpose was to test the adults. EYPTs therefore do not try to understand the toddler's endeavours, but interpret them as an attempt to push the boundaries. The adult's reaction is therefore to stop the toddler and set boundaries for their actions. It is also not uncommon for these kinds of 'negative' expectations to be associated with certain toddlers, who are then met with less openness and interest by the EYPTs.

Toddlers are human beings

If we assume that toddlers are human beings, this means that we assume that, in the same way as ourselves, they need to be able to act according to their own intentions, to be understood and to be met with care and affection. This requires different social conventions to those that we use if we think that young toddlers are irrational and their actions are random. The Swedish EYPTs who regarded the toddlers as human beings showed that they were 'focused on the toddlers' experiences' (Johansson, 2013). This meant that they listened to the toddlers' expressions, even though these were often only sounds and gestures, and they tried to interpret and confirm them. They also showed 'respect for the toddlers' desires' (Johansson, 2013). For example, when a toddler expressed that they did not want to answer the adult's question, the EYPT might drop the question. The toddlers were allowed to determine how much of themselves they were prepared to reveal to others, thereby protecting their integrity. However, respect is not synonymous with the idea that an adult should always go along with a toddler's wishes. It is more about showing that they understand the toddler's wishes and want to come to an agreement with the toddler. For example, if a toddler wanted to continue playing rather than come in and eat their lunch, the EYPT might have a friendly chat with them about what they were playing with, and then helping the toddler up, and they would both sit down to eat.

This is about prioritising the toddler's individuality, because 'toddlers should be able to be themselves' (Johansson, 2013). The

EYPTs endeavour to find a balance between the collective and the individual. For example, the cloakroom situation could create a dilemma when it is time for all the toddlers to go outside; some will not want to go outside, but they all have to. Of course, there could be very good reasons for a toddler not to want to go outside, and the EYPT's task would then be to find out the reasons behind this resistance. It is not always possible for the adults to find out what is causing the resistance, but it means something to the toddler that they have been approached by an adult who has tried to understand the toddler's perspective. Interacting with a toddler like a human being also means 'giving the toddler control' by allowing them to participate in decisions that concern themselves (Johansson, 2013). In other words, the EYPTs allow toddlers to do things in their own way, even though it is not the correct way. For example, a toddler might put their boots on the wrong feet and will not comply with the adult's suggestion to swap them over. EYPTs who make it a priority to allow toddlers to create their own experiences will accept the toddler's decision. For them, the most important thing is for the toddler to feel that they can have an influence on what is happening.

The toddler's perspective

As we have seen from Johansson's presentation of the three different views of the toddler as a person, the EYPT's view plays an essential role in determining how much account adults should take of toddlers' needs, intentions and wishes. Let us now look at this from the toddlers' perspective. What does it feel like for them, and what significance can this have for their perception of themselves as a person? Some toddlers will frequently feel that their expressions are met with benevolent interest and that their voice will be heard. On the one side, this will strengthen a toddler's confidence in their own initiative, but on the other side, it may also help to develop a very strong sense of individualism, which can weaken the toddler's sensitivity towards peers in the group. Other toddlers will experience that their emotional expressions and opinions are often ignored and seldom regarded as important. They often feel that they are the object of somebody else's will. According to Daniel Stern, even infants generalise their repeated experiences of interactions with their caregiver, and these repeated perceptions form the basis for the child's self-perception (Stern, 1985).

It is not about individual incidents, but the significance of what happens on an everyday basis in encounters between the toddler and the adult. Repeated experiences of being ignored or misunderstood can result in a reduction in the toddler's self-esteem, a feeling of inferiority and doubt in their own abilities.

The description we have given here is based on some categorisations that do not entirely correspond to the complexity of what takes place in the educational activities in an early years setting. Most toddlers will feel that they are treated with respect, are sometimes ignored and very occasionally affronted. These experiences are common to all mankind, and are also familiar to ourselves as adults. The challenge for EYPTs is to find a balance between consideration for the toddler's life here and now and consideration for the toddler's future, and between the child's right to participate and the child's need for protection. This is a dilemma that is part of our work as an EYPT.

♻ REFLECTION 6.3

Questions for team discussion:

» What view of the toddler as a person is important to us?

» How do we talk with and about the toddler?

» In which way do we adapt our work to the diverse intentions, needs, experiences and interests of the toddler?

Toddler's community and expressions in play

Being a teacher and caregiver for toddlers is demanding, because it means that we have to relate to people who are at a different stage of their lives compared to us adults. They are newcomers to the world who are just beginning to experience and explore the world around them. As already mentioned, play and interactions with peers are activities that children appear to value greatly. Adults' views on toddlers can inhibit or promote toddlers' development through play. There has been a change in the understanding of toddler's play – from egocentric play and parallel play (e.g. Piaget) towards toddlers' engagement and competence in social play.

To be able to support toddlers' play and toddlers as subjects, we need knowledge about toddlers' play. We will therefore present some of the research about toddlers' play in Nordic early years settings. Several of these studies use the theory of Merleau-Ponty. All of the studies could be described as interpreted qualitative research, and they have a common ground in using observation as a method and doing research *in* the early years setting. We think it is important to notice that this research (also based on choice of theory/metatheory) represent only *one* of several interpreted realities.

We have divided the research about toddlers' play based in the following topics: peer-communication, play routines, friendships, and negotiations and conflicts. Each topic is followed by a reflective guideline and questions that practitioners could use for team discussion. Even if we divide into different topics, we think it is important to notice that previous research indicates that these topics also should be viewed as a whole and as everyday aspects of toddlers' communication and play in the early years setting (e.g. Rosell, 2016).

Toddler's peer-communication

Several studies emphasise the lived body, or toddlers as body subjects, when they describe toddlers' peer-communication. Through being a body, human beings (both toddlers and adults), are in a continuous communication with the surroundings in the early years setting. The body holds previous experiences (e.g. about other body subjects and play materials), it lives in the present/in the moment, and through time moving towards a future. Based on this theory about the lived body, toddlers communicate in the setting and engage in play, both alone and in common play with each other. Toddlers' play is always about something, according to Løkken (2000). This something is bodily expressions and movements, the use of the room, and the use and engagement in small and big objects/materials. In toddlers' play with each other, this something could be described as a 'third party' (e.g. Løgstrup, 2010; Skjervheim, 2001). Someone takes an initiative (Merleau-Ponty, 2002) and an encounter occurs when the toddlers aim towards each other and respond to different initiatives (Rosell, 2016).

Engdahl (2011) has studied toddlers' communication in a Swedish setting and her findings indicate that the toddlers use bodily movement, gestures, their voices and facial expressions to invite other toddlers in play. The toddlers express methods as greeting, observing, attuning, taking others' perspectives and taking turn in peer communications. In an Icelandic toddler group, Pálmadóttir (2015) has studied how toddlers use their gaze, toys, repeated to-and-from movements with toys or sitting down next to another toddler to communicate that they want to initiate some play with them. Similar findings have been emphasised in different studies in Norwegian settings, where also repetition of peers' expressions, variations and the use of humour seem to be central in toddlers' peer-communication (e.g. Greve, 2008; Løkken, 2000; Rosell, 2016).

Toddlers' use of toys or objects, both as a form of inspiration for others and as a common 'third party' in play, have been a central finding in several studies. An understanding of toddlers' encounter and use of toys/objects is based on the understanding of the lived body and toys/objects as phenomenon, where toys/objects together with bodily expressions and the room create activities/play. Toddlers express meaning by behaving or getting involved in a particular way, where things/objects/activities may have particular meanings that result in particular actions (Johansson, 1999). Things/objects/ activities may be of different significance to children, and some will appear more appealing than others (Bengtsson, 2013). This can lead to a common ground and common play, but it also gives an understanding of toddlers' exploration and engagement in objects when playing alone. Gadamer (1989) refers to an understanding of 'play', in which there does not necessarily need to be a fellow player, but there must be something to play with, to provide counter play. Gadamer (1989) refers to the example of a cat playing with a ball of wool, in which the object (ball of wool) creates tension, variation and becomes a fellow player in the game. The basis for toddlers' involvement with things/ objects and their activities is the body. Objects can then be understood as a part of the body and the body's expression. The challenge is to support and safeguard the content that emerges in the toddler's expression with regard to objects and the activities that are created. It also challenges the adults in the setting in how they use and decorate the room with objects, and what objects they offer to the toddlers.

Reflective guideline 1

Toddlers' peer-communications

- Toddlers use the body for expression: mimicry, gestures, gaze, movement, sounds, words, the body's position in the room and by using small and big objects.
- Toddlers greet, observe, tune in, take the other's perspective and execute turn taking in their communication with peers.
- Imitation and repetition of peers' expressions, as well as variations, are central in toddlers' interaction with peers.
- Humour, joking and joyful shouts are prominent in the communication.
- Toddlers may seek out another toddler for several reasons: because of the activities created by peers, activities created by the use of certain objects or the objects this toddler is holding in its hand. Eventually it might just be that this toddler comes into their sight.
- Toddlers may offer toys/objects as an act of invitation (an initiative) to joined activity.
- Toddlers express initiatives in their communication with peers in order to create shared activities. The degree of initiative and openness to peers' initiatives creates different and varied interactions among toddlers. A summary of several studies of toddlers' communication with peers (especially two- to three-year-olds), identifies the following characteristics (even if some toddlers tend to be stuck in a specific characteristic, previous research indicates the dynamic by toddlers' alteration of the different characteristics in their encounters):
  - Toddlers show high competence in taking initiatives and openness in accepting that peers may take initiatives (peers' input) and in following up these inputs. The interaction is featured by mutual and interactive construction of the activity, a kind of reciprocity.
  - Toddlers show high competence in taking initiatives, but they are less open or attentive to peers' initiatives.
  - Toddlers show high competence in confirming and coming into line with peers' initiatives, but they seldom take own initiatives.
  - One of the toddlers seems to rule and organise the activity. The interaction is vulnerable, conflicts might occur and frequent shifts of initiatives to different activities might occur.
  - Toddlers are to a high degree occupied with their own activities, they are interacting with adults or they are walking around in the room (often carrying different objects). They seldom seek out peers.

Questions
- Have you observed some of these different kinds of interaction amongst the toddlers in your setting?
- How can you support toddlers' peer-communications?

(Engdahl, 2011; Greve, 2007; Johansson, 1999; Løkken, 2000; Michélsen, 2004; Rosell, 2016)

Toddlers' play routine

Using Merleau-Ponty's theory and her own observations in Norwegian settings, Gunvor Løkken (2000) has created the term 'the playful quality of the toddling style'. She describes the characteristics of this play in relation to the toddler's playful mentality (they 'are' playful), their here-and-there movements, their slapstick-style humour and the quality of the many recurrences. She interprets a playful 'glee concert',[1] performed by seven toddlers as a co-operative concert with no adult conductor. Toddlers' play is typified by a certain amount of chaos, in which the body is a key element. Løkken also shows how even the youngest children use their bodies to express themselves, when they are greeting and seeking peers, and when they set up and hold meetings with others. Løkken (2000) also refers to Stambak and Verba (1986) and their description of how toddlers create a mutual understanding without using words, by: (a) expressing an idea, (b) the other(s) understanding this fully or partly and expressing their agreement with the idea, (c) this response provoking an agreement from the other(s), (d) the interaction continuing with various suitable responses, but the basis of these recurrences and variations is the initially expressed idea. According to Løkken (2000), over time this can develop into play routines and a distinct toddler culture.

---

1 'Group glee' is a similar term describing this kind of phenomenon observed in toddler groups. It is characterised by joyful screaming, laughing and intense physical acts which occurred in simultaneous bursts or which spread in a contagious fashion from one child to another (Sherman, 1975).

Reflective guideline 2

Toddlers' play routine

- How toddlers create common (play) routines:
  - Somebody expresses an idea.
  - Peers understand this idea totally or partially and react according to the idea.
  - This answer creates respect and response from peers.
  - The interaction continues with recurrences and variations, but the basis of these recurrences and variations is the initially expressed idea.
- Those recurring interactions may develop into different toddler routines.
- Toddlers create these routines by using the body, the room and things (often big objects).
- The toddlers often express joy and excitement – usually accompanied by laughter and loud shouts.
- Examples of these kind of routines:
  - Running routines – Toddlers run back and forth in the room (from one wall to the other), or around a table, with or without objects, in a repeated pattern (a routine).
  - Mattress routines – Toddlers are actively using big mattresses. The toddlers use the mattress, their bodies and eventually the room in a repeating pattern (a routine).
  - Jumping routines – Toddlers jump from benches, chairs, sofas, etc. to the floor or a mattress. They use objects, the room and body in a repeated pattern.
- Toddler routines often appear as open activities – independent of the number of peers or their age.
- Toddler routines are created and developed by the children. They are the toddlers' own initiatives and expressions, collaboratively created with peers.

Questions
- Which play routines have you observed toddlers creating in your setting?
- How can we support the development of different play routines and why are they important?

(Løkken, 2000)

Friendship among toddlers

Friendships and the beginning of friendships can be described as a personal aspect of the 'third party' in encounters between toddlers. Greve (2007) has studied two-year-old children in a Norwegian setting, and how toddlers over time express their friendships with each other. Both Greve (2007) and Jonsdottir (2007) point out that the term friendship is another dimension of being together or a relationship.

Friendship is characterised as a mutual relationship where the children express common feelings about each other (Jonsdottir, 2007). Friendship indicates expressions for equality and joint interest and that the relation is based on voluntariness and the toddlers' expression of a joint 'We' (Greve, 2007). Friendships among toddlers are created over time through daily interactions/encounters in the setting. Friendship is an intersubjective experience and there are several kinds of expressions for friendships. In Greve's study the toddlers expressed a joint We by: creating meaning together, relating to each other's lifeworld, using humour, using the body, shared expressions of morality, and by protecting their relationship. Friendships are a more personal dimension of just being together; a friendship is the personal aspect of being together about something, and the development of friendships can be related to the EYPT's understanding and ability to facilitate this development.

Reflective guideline 3

Friendship amongst toddlers

- The term friendship includes a dimension that goes beyond the being together.
- Friendship includes a historic dimension based upon the past, the here-and-now and is pointing ahead. In other words, friendship needs time to develop.
- Hallmarks of friendship: expressions for equality, joint interest, relations based on voluntariness and expressions of a joint 'We'.
- A joint 'We' may be expressed by creating meaning together, relating to each other's lifeworld, using humor, shared expressions of morality (right-wrong, positive-negative) or by protecting/maintaining the relation within/against the peer group.
- Different types of friendship relations with different content of the joint 'We' can be found.
- Friendship relations may be dyads, triads, and so on.
- Hallmarks of friendships are especially visible from the age of two.

Questions

- Are there established or developing friendships in your group of toddlers?
- How can/do you support friendships between toddlers?

(Greve, 2007, 2008)

Toddlers' negotiations

Taking the other person's perspective into account, reciprocity or taking turns, being a guide – through bodily expressions, objects and the room – appear to be important aspects of toddlers' encounters and play. Some of the studies on toddlers' encounters have also emphasised that these encounters can be characterised as negotiations, disagreements, conflicts, frustrations and rejections/protection (Alvestad, 2010; Johansson, 1999; Rosell, 2016). It may be particularly in these cases, where the dialectic between the vulnerable and the competent toddler tends to become prominent, that the need for support from adults becomes apparent.

Johansson (1999), who studied how toddlers expressed ethics – what is worthy of pursuit (positive or negative and right or wrong) – refers to the toddlers' expressions of rights, both in terms of an expressed right to things/objects and an expressed right to share or protect valued relationships with others. The findings of protection of personal relationships and friendships are also supported in more recent research (Greve, 2007; Rosell, 2016). Løkken (2000) emphasises how small objects can lead to conflicts and disagreements during toddlers' interactions with each other. Rosell (2016) refers to similar findings as Løkken. Rosell (2016) also argues that conflicts and protections may have their background in toddlers' expressions of the right to play alone and their expressions to safeguard personal privacy and avoid violations (e.g. being afraid, blow, kick, be spit on, etc.). Skånfors, Löfdahl and Hägglund (2009) describe how toddlers actively uses the room to pull away in order to protect activities and relationships. There are also findings that indicate that elder children (two to three years of age) reject the youngest, and that rejection could be based on the children's seniority in the early years setting (Pálmadóttir, 2015).

Alvestad (2010) has studied toddlers' negotiations in play. In this study, it emerges that toddlers negotiate about relationships, the content of their interactions and material objects, both within dyads and between small groups of peers. Therefore, disagreements, conflicts and negotiations appear to be part of toddlers' everyday encounters with each other in a kindergarten. The challenge is to support and safeguard the toddlers' expressions and rights in these situations.

Reflective guideline 4

Toddlers' negotiations and conflicts

- Toddlers can express different rights in their communication with peers.
- Toddlers can express their right to things/objects in order to protect their personal activity or activity in a group.
- Toddlers can express their right to things/objects in order to protect their relations.
- Toddlers can express their right to personal and common space, a specific area in the room.
- Toddlers' disagreements can occur within a dyad (me-you).
- Toddlers' disagreements can occur when a dyad interact with other toddlers of the group (we-them).
- When toddlers negotiate and express agreement, the negotiations include imitation, variation, taking turns, turning of heads, gaze and the body's position as well as inter-subjectivity/taking the perspective of the other.
- When toddlers negotiate and express disagreement, the negotiations might include power, control and manipulation.
- Conflicts and peer rejection among toddlers can be based on protecting activities and/or relations, protecting space, protecting personal integrity, protecting objects/toys, age and seniority.

Questions
- How do different toddlers negotiate during playtime?
- How can you support negotiations and conflicts in toddlers' play?

(Alvestad, 2010; Johansson, 1999; Rosell, 2016)

EYPTs' experiences, reflections and strategies from England, Norway and Spain

ENGLAND

Tom Maybey from Kew, Mortlake, Barnes East Sheen Children's Centres, Achieving for Children, London

Out of all the ideas and recommendations that the Toddler Wellbeing (ToWe) Project has made me think and reflect on, I believe what I have learned about toddlers' voices and expressions to be the most significant.

Learning about the transactional model of interactions has made me look anew at the way we as practitioners interact with children and also the parents. And, as I work in a children's centre where parents and other carers stay with their children while on site, I have a revised understanding of interactions between children and their parents and the same children and practitioners.

I was familiar with the UN Convention on the Rights of the Child, and how all children should have the right to expression and to be heard, and the ToWe Project has made me think about how to give all children who attend our setting these rights. A large part of what a children's centre does is to try and get parents and carers who attend our groups with their children to have a greater understanding of how their little ones grow and develop. So after trying to impart this knowledge to the adults through displays, leaflets and both formal and informal conversations, I am now pleased to see that they are more aware of the ways their child may have a 'voice' and have desires and wants, even if they are pre-verbal. Some of the leaflets and flyers I have made have been about letting your child make simple choices at snack time, or about the importance of being face to face while playing and communicating so that the adult begins to recognise the more subtle non-verbal messages their child may be displaying.

I have tried to create more opportunities for children of all ages to make choices and have a say in the way the sessions are planned and facilitated. The Early Years Foundation Stage (EYFS) requires that we use the interests of children to plan activities, and we also have as many resources as possible stored in easily accessible containers – that are labeled with photos wherever possible – so the children in attendance can choose what they want to play with should it not be initially available. And the resources that get chosen in this way are often factored into the planning for the following session.

I have tried to capture the children's voices and expressions in the displays I have made for the centre. Putting up examples of children's work and accompanying them with captions that are direct quotes from the children who made them – and, most importantly, highlighting these to the adults, so they begin to understand the importance of valuing their children's voices and opinions. In a recent termly 'Stay and Play' session evaluation I added a few questions that directly asked parents and carers about the ToWe Project and wellbeing. And while – perhaps unfortunately – only 6 of the 35 responses said they were aware of our work with the ToWe Project, 27 out of 35 said that attending the centre had provided them with new ideas for things they can do at home to promote wellbeing in their children. And, through further conversation, it has emerged that a lot of parents have gone on to give their children more choices, more say in family life, and added respect and dignity to their children's opinions.

NORWAY

Maj Gabrielsen from Sandvedhaugen Barnehage, Sandnes Kommune, Sandnes

We started this with the following goal: to improve staff knowledge and awareness of toddlers' own voices and expressions.

At our kindergarten, we have decided to focus on play, as we believe that, alongside language, play is the children's natural way of communicating with each other. We wanted the staff to observe, reflect and be aware of what toddlers are expressing through play: facial expressions, body language, sounds and words. It is important that we respect these statements as meaningful communication between the toddlers. When we decided to focus on play in particular, it was logical for us to include the role of adult in this context. Every week, assistants received training in which we spent much of the time reflecting on the role of adult and participation in play. The management group at the kindergarten have also reflected on this output during management meetings.

It was important for the staff to reflect on different views of toddlers. Who am I as an adult when I play with the toddlers? Am I the adult who knows best and who acts based on what I know is in the best interests of the children and therefore do not need to consider the toddlers' way of seeing things? Am I the adult who believes that toddlers are irrational and that toddlers act without the ability to experience and create meaning, with the aim of testing the adult, or am I someone who sees toddlers as fellow human beings and therefore realises that toddlers also demonstrate a need to act based on their own intentions and opinions and to be received and understood in a good and loving way? During this training, we concluded that we want to see toddlers as fellow human beings.

We stressed that adults should observe the toddlers' play both inside and outside and then draw up strategies for the direct and indirect involvement of adults in play. We became more aware of the physical environment and how play and relationships between children were facilitated (e.g. deStefano and Mueller, 1982). The EYPT created small play corners and provided relevant equipment as a source of inspiration in play. However, where we can see potential for improvement is the amount of equipment and toys we have out at any time. If we put too much out, there may be too strong a focus on play equipment, which might then take away the focus from the toddlers' relationships with each other. The room could also easily become cluttered if there are too many toys scattered across the floor. We can also see potential for improvement with regards to how we offer toys and equipment to the toddlers. Are the toys too high up for them to get hold of? Are the dolls in a pile or in a box? And can the toddlers choose for themselves which toys they prefer?

We also reflected on how we as EYPTs should support and take part in the play. We use the direct strategies mentioned in the educational tool 'Toddlers' voice and expressions' (e.g. Spotlight, chain, catalyst, rubber band, interpreter, regulator and guide; Os, 2004).

Through observation and small stories (narratives), we have been able to see how toddlers communicate in play. The very youngest children use a lot of body language, noises and facial mimicry, while the slightly older ones who have more verbal language often use words in order to agree on what and how they should play. The oldest children at the kindergarten (three to five years) use more advanced language along with play strategies such as negotiation, planning and switching in and out of roles.

What are we left with after having worked with this output?

We have also decided to use the educational tool amongst children in the three to five age group. We have witnessed changes while observing both the oldest and the youngest children. The EYPTs are more aware of what they can observe in children's play. We find that children, particularly the oldest ones, have become more attentive towards each other. The children have found peace and calm and they happily take part in the play. We can also see that the children are playing more across age groups and are playing well. In addition, we have observed the language the children use between themselves. We consider play to be our most important educational tool and try to ensure that the indoor group facilities and the outdoor area invite children to play.

Some EYPTs find that visible adults and physical and mental presence have a positive impact on the children's play.

An educational leader states the following:
The role of EYPTs

What do the observation findings mean for the role of adults in play both indoors and outdoors?

By using an evaluation form, we have become more aware of what is actually happening during play, as well as the impact that we as adults could have on toddlers' play and their wellbeing during play. We already knew a lot before, but it is always good to have a refresher. We were already focusing on outdoor play and our study has reaffirmed that being an active adult outdoors means a great deal for toddlers' play environment. Indoors, we have become better at being on the floor, albeit not always playing with the toddlers, but at least nearby. It reassures the toddlers that if something were to happen, help is at hand.

Initiatives

What initiatives have been implemented within the group?

Within the group, we have made some basic materials (such as toys, pearls, drawing materials, etc.) more accessible for the toddlers. This has freed up time for the adults, as we do not have to be interrupted and asked for help getting certain materials down. We have also noticed toddlers tidying up after themselves on their own initiative, but of course, they sometimes need a reminder. We split into small groups when we have time, which we believe makes the day more harmonious for everyone.

Evaluation

'We will continue to leave the materials out for the toddlers; while in the long term, we will introduce additional materials (dare we bring out the wet paints?). Being able to access materials increases the feeling of mastery amongst the toddlers, as they find that they become proud that they can look after things. We will also continue to be on the floor and split into small groups when we can.'

Another educational leader talks about the initiatives that have been implemented within the group:

- Presence: raising awareness of our choices and justifications (ongoing process).

- Spread ourselves around the rooms, take part/be available to the toddlers, indoors and outdoors.

- Split the rooms into nooks and crannies where toddlers can enjoy their activities.

- Identify the toddlers' initiatives and reflect on what the toddlers need from us.

- Stay in the background and observe/release the toddlers' initiative.

- Support the toddlers who are struggling most to develop good relations.

- In connection with conflict resolution – safeguard all parties.

- Improvise and be able to offer more time when play is going well.

The pedagogical leader of a toddler group says that she has started involving the parents in the toddlers' play more. What used to be called 'Parents' Coffee Time' is now called 'Stay and Play' (inspired by the 'Achievement for Children' programme). The staff and parents sit down on the floor together with the toddlers during the play session. The EYPTs tell the parents what the toddlers are learning in the different play situations.

In the future, we will continue to be aware of our view of toddlers and the children's right to express themselves. One of the key aspects for us of course is how we adults perceive, relate to and meet toddlers in play situations.

SPAIN

Mireia Miralpeix Anglerill and Mª Àngels Domènech Pou from Mas Balmanya Escola Bressol Pública, Surara Serveis, Cataluña

The ToWe Project content on toddlers' voice and expressions has equipped us with a conceptual framework and a platform from which we can analyse our interventions and make the meaningful, as well as observe the toddlers and interpret their interactions.

It has helped us become aware of what the toddlers are expressing through play and identify new elements that arise in their interactions. We have also been able to expand our perspective and question our own interventions as EYPTs. It has helped us become more mindful, not only of what we say but also of what we do.

Before working on the content on toddlers' voice and expressions, we set out to describe real situations in which we believed adult intervention was needed, what action had been taken, whether it was direct or indirect, and what the toddlers' reactions were. The vast majority of situations posed by the team referred to conflicts, and direct intervention depended on the toddlers' ability to solve conflicts or the possibility of them harming themselves. After reading the material, we are able to better identify what a direct and indirect intervention means, as well as the fact that the range of possible interventions in toddlers' interactions is much broader.

In relation to the toddlers, we have begun to consider what the types of interaction that arise in play express. We had not seen it from that perspective until then, and it opened up a major new sphere of knowledge (research and reflection) to us.

We have started recording playtime situations and analysing them in our team meetings, both interactions among toddlers and our own attitudes and interventions and how they can influence the toddlers' interactions. We can listen to a toddler in a different way and incorporate all their language.

This effort has mainly allowed us to become aware of the richness of the interactions that occur among the toddlers and what they mean. As a result, we are now able to modify our attitudes and interventions, if needed. There has been a change in our perspective and our listening.

One example of this is when some toddlers run through the classroom in a line, following a given route. In this situation, the discourse of the EYPT associated with this play was 'these toddlers aren't playing; they're just running through the classroom and distorting the entire dynamic'. When, after reading the ToWe Project material, we were able to dig deeper and assign a meaning and significance to this kind of behaviour and understand that this is a play routine in which a given kind of interaction emerges, our way of thinking and speaking, and even our interventions, changed. We no longer view it as something to stop and instead may encourage toddlers to do it in another place or at another time.

Now, it is no longer the toddlers who distort the dynamic, who don't know how to play! We have incorporated a much more respectful view of the toddlers which generates debate in the team and leads us to reconsider our own intervention!

Conclusion: experiences from setting partners on the ToWe Project

Our aim with this chapter was to offer a political, theoretical and empirical view on the adult role, toddlers' expressions and toddlers' play, and provide an opportunity to discuss this knowledge in the team settings through reflective guidelines and questions. In this chapter, we offered a theoretical framework for *one* understanding of toddlers' 'being-in-the-world', how they communicate and engage in activities with things/object and other body–subjects, exemplified and concretised through findings from empirical research. The theoretical framework and the empirical examples are meant as 'a way to think about' and reflect on how to support toddlers' expressions in play. The reflective guidelines and questions have been used by practitioners, teachers and setting partners in the ToWe Project. After using the material for a period some of the practitioners and teachers expressed a change in the adults' attitudes in playtime through being more 'with' the child, sitting close to the toddlers and supporting their interactions in play. Others express a changing view of toddlers' 'noise' and 'running around' and a consciousness about how they display objects/materials in the setting. One practitioner describes that:

> Through using the reflective guidelines we have become more aware of the content in toddlers' play and the importance of us adults in play and the wellbeing in play. We find that the toddlers have become more responsive to each other and that they have found a calm and contentment in their play.

References

Alvestad, T. (2010) *Barnehagens relasjonelle verden: Små barn som kompetente aktører i produktive forhandlinger* (vol. 294). Göteborg: Acta Universitatis Gothoburgensis.

Bae, B. (2010) 'Realizing children's right to participation in early childhood settings: Some critical issues in a Norwegian context.' *Early Years, 30*, 3, 205–218.

Bengtsson, J. (2005) *Med livsvärlden som grund: Bidrag till utvecklandet av en livsvärldsfenomenologisk ansats i pedagogisk forskning.* Lund: Studentlitteratur.

Bengtsson, J. (2013) 'With the lifeworld as ground. A research approach for empirical research in education: The Gothenburg tradition.' *Indo-Pacific Journal of Phenomenology, 13*, 1–18. doi: 10.2989/IPJP.2013.13.2.4.1178.

Bowlby, J. (1969) *Attachment and Loss.* London: Hogarth Press.

Burleson, B.R., Delia, J.G. and Applegate, J.L. (1992) 'Effects of maternal communication and children's social-cognitive and communication skills on children's acceptance by the peer group.' *Family Relations, 41*, 264–272.

Corsaro, W.A. (1997) *The Sociology of Childhood.* Thousand Oaks, CA: Pine Forge Press.

deStefano, C. and Mueller, E. (1982) 'Environmental determinants of peers social activity in 18 month old males.' *Infant Behavior and Development, 5*, 175–183.

Engdahl, I. (2011) *Toddlers as Social Actors in the Swedish Preschool.* Stockholm: Department of Child and Youth studies, Stockholm University.

Gadamer, H.G. (1989) *Truth and Method*. London: Sheed & Ward.

Gopnik, A., Meltzoff, A.N. and Kuhl, P. (1999) *The Scientist in the Crib*. New York: HarperCollins Publisher.

Greve, A. (2007) *Vennskap mellom små barn i barnehagen* (vol. no. 89). Oslo: Unipub forlag.

Greve, A. (2008) 'Friendships and participation among young children in a Norwegian kindergarten.' In Berthelsen, D., Brownlee, J. and Johansson, E. (eds.) *Participatory learning in the early years. Research and pedagogy*. pp 78–92. London: Routledge.

Hazen, N.L. and Black, B. (1989) 'Preschool peer communications skills: The role of social statue and interaction context.' *Child Development, 60*, 867–876.

Johansson, E. (1999) *Etik i små barns värld: Om värden och normer bland de yngsta barnen i förskolan*. Göteborg: Acta Universitatis Gothoburgensis.

Johansson, E. (2013). Små barns læring. *Møter mellom barn og voksne i barnehagen*. Oslo: Gyldendal Akademisk.

Jonsdottir, F. (2007) *Barns kamratrelationer i förskolan: Samhörighet tillhörighet vänskap utanförskap* (vol. 35). Malmö: Området för lärarutbildning, Malmö högskola.

Løgstrup, K.E. (2010) *Den etiske fordring*. Århus: Klim.

Løkken, G. (2000) *Toddler peer culture: The social style of one and two year old body subjects in everyday interaction*. Pedagogisk institutt, Fakultet for samfunnsvitenskap og teknologiledelse, Norges teknisk-naturvitenskapelig universitet, Trondheim.

Merleau-Ponty, M. (2002) *Phenomenology of Perception*. London: Routledge.

Michélsen, E. (2004) *Kamratsamspel på småbarnsavdelingar* (vol. 128). Stockholm: Pedagogiska institutionen.

Os, E. (2004) 'Children under three: Teachers' support to peer-relations and play in day care centres.' Paper to the 23rd ICCP World Play Conference. 15–17 September 2004. Accessed on 30 January 2018 at www.iccp-play.org/documents/krakow/os.pdf

Pálmadóttir, H. (2015) *Communities in play: Young preschool children's perspectives on relationships, values and roles*. University of Iceland, School of Education, Reykjavik.

Rosell, Y. (2016) *Møter mellom barn – kontinuitet, dissonans og brudd i kommunikasjonen*. (Doktorgradsavhandling), Det humanistiske fakultet, Universitetet i Stavanger, Stavanger.

Sameroff, A.J. (1987) 'The social context of development.' In Eisenberg, N. (ed.) *Contemporary Topics in Developmental Psychology*. New York: Wiley.

Sherman, L.W. (1975) 'An ecological study of glee in small groups of preschool children.' *Child Development, 1*, 53–61.

Skånfors, L., Löfdahl, A. and Hägglund, S. (2009) 'Hidden spaces and places in the preschool: Withdrawal strategies in preschool children's peer culture.' *Journal of Early Childhood Research* Vol 7(1). pp 94–109. doi: 10.1177/1476718X08098356.

Skjervheim, H. (2001) *Deltakar og tilskodar og andre essays*. Oslo: Aschehoug.

Sommer, D. (2014) *Barndomspsykologi: Små barn i en ny tid* (2. utg.). Bergen: Fagbokforlaget.

Stambak, M. and Verba, M. (1986) 'Organization of social play among toddlers: An ecological approach.' *Process and Outcome in Peer Relationships*, 229–247.

Stern, D.N. (1985) *The Personal World of the Infant*. London: Karnac Books.

UN General Assembly (1989) *Convention on the Rights of the Child*, 20 November 1989, Treaty Series, 1577, 3. Accessed 2 October 2017 at www.refworld.org/docid/3ae6b38f0.html

UNCRC (2005) *Implementing Child Rights in Early Childhood*, 20 September 2006, CRC/C/GC/7/Rev.1. Accessed 2 October 2017 at www.refworld.org/docid/460bc5a62.html

UNCRC (2009) *The right of the child to be heard*, 20 July 2009, CRC/C/GC/12. Accessed 2 October 2017 at www.refworld.org/docid/4ae562c52.html

UNICEF UK (1989) *A summary of the UN Convention on the Rights of the Child.* Accessed 1 February 2016 at https://www.unicef.org.uk/wp-content/uploads/2010/05/UNCRC_summary-1.pdf

CHAPTER 7

EARLY LANGUAGES

Cristina Corcoll and Carme Flores

'Every child has the right to learn and use the language, customs and religion of their family, whether or not these are shared by the majority of the people in the country where they live.'

(UNICEF UK, 1989, Article 30)

Introduction

Early childhood education should provide toddlers with the best learning opportunities. Nowadays, when focusing on language and language learning, the best learning opportunities should include adapting the plurilingual approach to the toddlers' needs and abilities. The plurilingual approach looks at language and language learning in a complex and enriching way: the focus is not primarily placed on acquiring words but on acquiring a positive attitude towards learning words. That is, learning languages whilst developing the understanding that the languages that we are familiar with are not the only ones (nor the most important ones) in the world; beginning to hear and notice similarities and differences among the languages that surround us, and, ultimately developing interest and respect towards them.

As toddlers grow, the plurilingual approach, as well as its implementation in formal contexts, becomes more complex or technical but, in early ages, we like to talk about the 'pedagogy of diversity'. By this, we mean creating the right conditions in the setting for languages to be used by families and early years practitioners and teachers (EYPTs) as well as making them visible all around. Surrounding toddlers with diverse linguistic and cultural inputs may help them develop into the plurilingual, globalised speakers needed in today's world.

The link between diversity and identity construction is key here. We feel that a toddler's individual identity can be better developed by comparing it to other people's identities, and one element that can clearly help us here is language: the language spoken by a toddler, the language spoken by their friend at the setting, the language spoken by the practitioner, the language or languages used at home, and so on. Thus, making these languages (whether few or many) visible at the setting will be the first step to take.

♻ REFLECTION 7.1

Think about your definition of language and language learning. Which of the following do you agree with and why?

> » Learning languages is learning about new cultures, thus broadening our experience and understanding of the world.

> » Learning languages benefits learners at different levels: cognitive, emotional, social.

> » Learning languages is a key competence today.

> » Learning languages, if done well, is never damaging to the learning process.

Dealing with the languages that can play a role in an early years setting, we may distinguish between two realities. In Reality 1, the focus is on the toddlers' linguistic (and cultural) identities, that is, the languages that toddlers and their families use at home and which have, to a greater or lesser extent, an influence on the toddler's upbringing. In Reality 1, the setting should welcome these languages. In Reality 2, the focus is on the educational project of the setting that aims at using and developing an additional language. In some European countries, learning an additional language (English mostly) is a social demand: it has become a must for students to have an advanced level of the language by the time they leave school. This means that toddlers are starting to be exposed to the language at an earlier age and many settings need to find the best way to make this possible and beneficial for the toddlers and their learning process. Next, these two realities will be dealt with.

Reality 1: Welcoming toddlers' linguistic (and cultural) identities to the setting

Globalisation and immigration mean that, in many settings, pluri-lingualism is a reality: there are many toddlers whose home language (HL) is different from the setting's main language. Welcoming toddlers' linguistic and cultural identities to the setting means acknowledging and valuing their HLs, whilst offering toddlers the chance to learn and use the main social language.

The first step a setting should take in order to do this is to gather information regarding the linguistic diversity it has. It must be noted that the linguistic picture may be quite different depending on the country or the setting, or even comparing one year to another. This is why it is important to keep updating the data.

♻ REFLECTION 7.2

Reality 1: Identifying language diversity in the setting

What is the linguistic situation in your setting? Which is the social language? How many other languages are there?

The tool presented in Table 7.1 aims at helping obtain information regarding the language uses of families at home. Having this information is essential to providing good language practices at the setting. In fact, it is the first step towards improving language learning and use. Thus, we offer EYPTs the basis for a questionnaire to help them gather relevant information regarding toddlers' language repertoire.

♻ REFLECTION 7.3

Reality 1: Identifying language diversity in the setting

Think of the tool above as related to your setting. Does it include all the relevant aspects? Can the relevant information be easily collected and analysed?

Table 7.1 Reality 1 Questionnaire

Reality 1: Questionnaire to gather data regarding language diversity in the setting
Basic characteristics of the family
1. Family type (nuclear, reconstituted, lone-parent, extended family)
2. Education level (university studies, secondary education)
3. Ages of the members of the family
Perceptions towards the home language
1. Do you feel your home language should have a place at the setting? Why/why not?
2. How do you feel when you hear or see your home language at the setting? (e.g. proud, embarrassed, I do not feel anything)
3. Would you like to take part in early childhood education activities to learn more about the children's language acquisition process?
4. Would you like to co-operate with the setting to make your home language visible?
Use of the home language in the family
1. Are you provided with resources to support your toddler's linguistic development at home?
2. What type of linguistic activities do you do at home with your toddler? (e.g. read stories, listen to songs, sing songs, talk, etc.)
3. Which language is used at home with the toddler?
4. Who uses each language?
5. What is each language used for?

Welcoming toddlers' HLs at the setting is necessary if we are committed to offering a quality education to toddlers: adapting to toddlers and their circumstances and taking them into account is key. Following Siraj-Blatchford and Clarke (2011, p.22):

> When young children who speak a home language other than English start in the nursery or pre-school setting they begin the process of learning an additional language. Some of these children already speak more than one language. However, suddenly the language that they have used for their daily lives is no longer the language that they hear around them… Unless early childhood educators are familiar with the children's home language, social class background and culture, and provide a supportive environment, these toddlers are in danger of being marginalized and may experience an insecure and anxious start to their entry into nursery and schooling.

Specifically, welcoming HLs would help EYPTs:

- to *actively* respect all identities. Language is an essential part of identity: 'the way toddlers feel about themselves is not innate or inherited, it is learned' (Siraj-Blatchford and Clarke, 2011, p.3).

- to promote children's self-esteem. 'Positive self-esteem depends upon whether children feel that others accept them and see them as competent and worthwhile' (Siraj-Blatchford and Clarke, 2011, p. 3).

- to improve learning atmosphere. 'Researchers have shown the connection between academic achievement and self-esteem' (Siraj-Blatchford and Clarke, 2011, p.3).

- to create an inclusive culture (Mistry and Sood, 2015, p.14).

⟳ REFLECTION 7.4

Reality 1: Identifying language diversity in the setting

Think of the team of EYPTs at the setting. What is their linguistic background? Is it made visible? Is it used effectively to support toddlers and their families?

Toddlers' (and their families') linguistic realities can be welcomed to settings by promoting several strategies, as listed below:

- By collecting all linguistically-relevant information from families (Table 7.1 can be used).

- By making languages visible at the setting.

- By developing our own linguistic competence.

- By giving toddlers (and their families) opportunities to share their knowledge.

- By creating a stress-free environment where toddlers can use language.

- By using relevant pedagogical strategies (some will be addressed when dealing with Reality 2 below).

To assess how far the setting has gone in the way to make HLs visible at the setting, the rubric in Table 7.2 may be used. The internal evaluation done through this rubric can be the starting point to see how and where this aspect should be improved.

Table 7.2 Internal Evaluation for Improvement Rubric

Visibility of HLs at the setting	They are not visible	They are visible occasionally	They are clearly visible
Use of resources linked to HLs: photographs, books, information in different languages, objects and artifacts of different cultures	No resources are used	Some resources are used	A great diversity of resources is used
Effectiveness of resources linked to HLs to support language learning	They are not effectively used	They are used occasionally	They are effectively used
Sufficiency of resources in terms of quality	Insufficient	Sufficient	Excellent
Time devoted to HLs	No time is devoted	Some time is devoted	A lot of time is devoted
Activities done related to HLs: read stories in different HLs, sing songs in different HLs, give children (and their families) time to share their HLs	No activities are done	Some activities are done	Many activities are done
Engagement of children in HL activities: they show interest in listening to stories in HLs, they play with languages and show curiosity, they like to show what they know in other HLs	They are not engaged	They are engaged occasionally	They are very engaged
Engagement of families in HL activities: they bring materials in HLs, they are happy to participate in school activities	They are not engaged	They are engaged occasionally	They are very engaged
In-service training related to the visibility of HLs	No training offered	Training offered occasionally	A lot of training offered

🔁 REFLECTION 7.5

Reality 1: Identifying language diversity in the setting

Think of the tool, Table 7.2, as related to your setting. Does it include all the relevant aspects? Can the relevant information be easily collected and analysed?

Reality 2: Bringing new languages to the setting

When we talk about learning a new language in early childhood education, we do not mean acquiring a few words which may enable parents to be proud of their toddlers when asked to name five colours or to answer the question 'what's your name?' It means much more than singing a song at the end of the school or setting year or wearing a pumpkin mask at Halloween. Introducing an additional language means being consistent with the characteristics of the stage and, therefore, respectful of the educational principles which are at the basis of the process:

> Due to its interest and importance and because of the advantages of an early treatment, it is worth addressing some contents towards which children may not initially show interest, as may be the case of a second language. To do it, however, some educational principles need to be respected. (Paniagua and Palacios, 2005, p.20)

🔁 REFLECTION 7.6

Reality 2: Bringing new languages to the setting

Think of the five educational principles that underpin early childhood education in your context. Why do you think they are important when designing the implementation of an additional language project in the setting?

At the basis of these educational principles there is the need to create an environment rich in possibilities, rich in language and which stimulates acquisition. We should aim at providing meaningful communicative experiences, appropriate for the toddler's pace, interests and needs, which will take place in many immersion opportunities in an additional language (Flores and Corcoll, 2008).

Language is an instrument for developing different capacities, for interacting with the world around us and with other people, for expressing feelings, for experimenting, for playing, for beginning to understand complexity. We communicate through different languages, and we will do the same with the additional language. The only challenge will be the toddler's communicative limitations, which will require specific strategies that support understanding. The naturalness of the continuous use of the language in an immersion environment means that toddlers will gradually see using the language as something useful and meaningful.

Therefore, there is the need for the adult who brings the additional language to the setting to be an early childhood education practitioner, highly proficient in the language in all its complexity, so that language can be used fluently and accurately in any communicative opportunity. The language that will be used by the adult is not an object of study, but a means to communicate spontaneously, that is, naturally, and above all, frequently.

♻ REFLECTION 7.7

Reality 2: Bringing new languages to the setting
Think of some teaching strategies that you think would be effective in an additional language immersion context. In which ways could they be used and when? Are they very different from the teaching strategies you could use in your first language with your toddlers?

In order to bring a new language to the setting, there are a number of communicative strategies that may be considered by practitioners:

1. Habit and routines become rich learning opportunities. Getting children to *live* a new language necessarily entails taking advantage of the everyday moments that arise outside of the more guided sessions that might be included within the setting schedule. These moments can be longer or shorter and action-filled or passive, but in any case they should include the daily routines that make up everyday activities at the setting. By this we mean times that can range from washing their hands before eating to walking students outside to the playground (Flores and Corcoll, 2011). Referred to as O'CLILS, Outdoor Content Language Integrated Learning at School/Settings.

2. Providing information talk is useful and beneficial. The role of the adult who brings the additional language to the classroom is fundamentally the role of a mediator, that is, the one who mediates (linguistically) between the child's actions and the verbal description of the action. Using information talk effectively will allow the child to interiorise sensorial, motor and symbolic action schemes (Paniagua and Palacios, 2005, p.67).

3. Routine chants and games promote participation and interaction, whether verbally or non-verbally. These strategies engage toddlers in their daily routines; at the same time, music and movement help them integrate language and meaning through rhythm and action and provide an important socialisation element at the setting.

4. The use of visuals supports understanding and captures toddlers' attention. Visuals elements such as pictures, realia, photographs and posters, among others, help practitioners bring the real world into the setting, thus making learning meaningful and more exciting (Brinton, 2001). They are also helpful providers of variety for diverse learning styles and facilitate language development by making it more authentic and more integral.

5. Scaffolding language through rephrasing (expanding/ improving toddlers' oral productions) and recasting (providing toddlers with their utterances translated into the additional language) improves toddlers' readiness to participate, to interact and thus to become more confident through their language development. Scaffolding language should be consistently used in the setting, in order to guarantee interaction and communicative flow.

6. Repetition and modelling also become key strategies that support understanding. Practitioners should think of how repetition of key language can be naturally provided in the different interaction moments with the toddlers. The use of body language also becomes key for supporting meaning, understanding and helping toddlers gain confidence.

7. Finally, it is important to bear in mind that interactions based on smiles and a positive attitude are, among others, examples of golden opportunities that the practitioner should take advantage of.

To assess how far the setting has gone to introduce new languages, the observation tool, Table 7.3 may be used.

Table 7.3 O'CLILS Observation Sheet

O'CLILS Observation Sheet				
O'CLILS Moment				
Time of the day				
Duration				
Number of Toddlers				
Number of EYPTs	EYPTs using Additional Language		EYPTs using L1 (First Language)	
STRATEGIES	NEVER: Not observed	RARELY: Rarely observed	SOMETIMES: Observed but occasionally	OFTEN/ ALWAYS: Regularly observed
Use of routines				
Use of information talk				
Use of scaffolding techniques				
Use of songs and routine chants				
Use of visuals (e.g. pictures, frames, realia)				
Use of 'golden opportunities' for interaction				

Use of repetition				
Use of modelling				

⟳ REFLECTION 7.8

Reality 2: Bringing new languages to the setting

Think of the tool, Table 7.3, as related to your setting. Does it include all the relevant aspects? Can you reflect upon how these strategies are developed? Can you provide specific examples to support your reflection?

EYPTs' experiences, reflections and strategies from England, Norway and Spain

ENGLAND

Tom Maybey from Kew, Mortlake, Barnes and East Sheen Children's Centres, Achieving for Children, London

I had been working with toddlers for nine years when I began participating in the ToWe Project, and had attended many training courses on children's language and development. What the ToWe Project recommendations have helped me to do is to reflect on my previously acquired knowledge with a new understanding of how all languages – not just the one(s) they use at home – benefit the wellbeing of toddlers who attend my setting.

The ToWe Project materials – most specifically the setting audit – have helped me to make sure that my setting (which is a children's centre in South West London) and my practice are as language-rich as possible.

I have used more multilingual words when creating displays and resources, as the ToWe Project materials suggest that doing so both benefits children who understand that language, but also exposure to new languages is a learning experience for all children. And, as parents and carers are present with the children in our setting, the multilingual resources are as much for them to feel welcomed and included as they are for their children.

In creating and sourcing these resources, I researched about what non-English languages were most spoken amongst centre users. The results yielded a few surprises, and there were a few languages that I was not expecting to see there. This has given me new insight into the families who attend our centre, and provided me with new countries and cultures to celebrate in our activities.

The ToWe Project materials also highlight the importance of being patient, tolerant and flexible when dealing with communicating with toddlers. Having these recommendations at the front of my mind during children's centre sessions has been very important for me, as we have found through our own research that parents and carers who attend the centre learn from the practitioners' interactions with children, and try to do the same with their own children. So if the ToWe Project materials are influencing my practice for the better, then they will also be beginning to influence the way that parents and carers interact with their own children at home.

The materials and recommendations stress the importance of valuing languages other than English (or whichever language is predominant in the setting), and this ties in to a very common question I am often asked by parents – won't speaking their home language be detrimental to their learning of English, and will their children learn language slower or get confused between multiple languages? The ToWe Project guidelines and materials have given me more information to use when reassuring parents that these possibilities are unlikely, and that being multilingual is a great asset for children to have.

I am looking forward to further implementing ToWe Project recommendations and sharing best practice with other practitioners who are also involved in the project. My involvement for the past fourteen months has yielded great improvements in my own practice, and I hope to further spread the knowledge that I have gained.

NORWAY

Maj Gabrielsen from Sandvedhaugen Barnehage, Sandnes Kommune, Sandnes

At Sandvedhaugen Barnehage (kindergarten), we work actively every year to learn through experiencing what it is like to have children from other countries and with a different mother tongue at the kindergarten. In the case of these children, it is necessary to take account of both linguistic and cultural factors. We have children from many different countries who have a mother tongue other than Norwegian.

In Sandnes municipality, when a child who does not understand Norwegian starts kindergarten, the setting can apply for bilingual assistance. We apply to the Centre for Multilingual Children and Young People (FBU).

Bilingual assistants help to integrate all children within the group into the community and help them understand and make themselves understood at the kindergarten. The assistants also act as bridge-builders and culture mediators between children with a minority language background and children with an ethnic Norwegian background, and help the kindergarten to establish good contact with the parents.

However, it is not always possible to obtain a bilingual assistant, as it depends on which mother tongue a bilingual assistant is needed for and whether there are any applicants for the position. It is also a question of finance. Since autumn 2016, the older children (four- and five-year-olds) have been given priority.

However, we have found that the very youngest children starting at kindergarten and their parents also need help understanding a typical Norwegian kindergarten day. In Sandnes municipality, kindergartens now work with each other. This is particularly important during the familiarisation period, when the child and their parents are at their most vulnerable if they do not speak Norwegian or have not been to a Norwegian kindergarten before. In these cases, kindergartens can 'lend' bilingual assistants to one another for the first two or three weeks.

We believe it is important to have a good initial discussion with parents from other countries. During this discussion, we use a form prepared by the FBU called initial discussion with minority language parents. If necessary, we use an interpreter during these discussions.

In this form, we may ask for information such as:

- the child's language at home

- what other languages the child speaks

- who the child speaks with in their mother tongue

- how long the child has lived in Norway

- anything about the child's language skills that the kindergarten should be aware of

- how do you stimulate your child's language skills at home, what does the child like to play with, friends and childhood culture?

We also talk a little about a typical kindergarten day.

In collaboration with the FBU, we also provide information explaining what a Norwegian kindergarten is and the importance of being able to use both one's mother tongue and Norwegian in everyday situations. There are folders for different mother tongues.

The staff at the kindergarten are responsible for linguistic development in Norwegian. It is important to note that this does not only happen in controlled language activities, but throughout the kindergarten day from the moment the children arrive until they are collected. We must consciously speak to the child throughout the day and the discussion must be meaningful. We aim to help the children develop cognitively, emotionally and socially. The child is not just a language, but a human being with their own opinions, needs and expressions. (The child might be a big brother, a singer, football player, etc.)

Learning a new language can be challenging and can take a long time. At our kindergarten, we believe it helps to use specifics and images at the same time as we use the language.

One of the staff's tasks is to help the children understand how they can create a link between the languages they have access to and put this link into context. Children do not need simple words, but language that means something at all times.

SPAIN

Natàlia Turmo and Sílvia Turmo from Petita Escola, Barcelona, Cataluña

At Petita Escola we believe in the richness that languages offer those who can understand and speak them. Catalan, Spanish and English co-exist in our society, and so they do in our school as well. Catalan and Spanish are the native languages of most of our students, and we introduce them to English as an additional language through their daily lives at school.

Learning English at early ages is a social necessity in our world; however, our motivation goes beyond this. We steadfastly believe, and have confirmed it with the training in the ToWe Project, that contact with additional languages fosters an open attitude towards learning other languages and cultures in children, and it develops in them an entire series of language-learning strategies, tools and skills in general.

English has been part of our day-to-day lives at our school from the very start. But it wasn't until we read and reflected on the ToWe Project handbooks that we decided to take a step further in this area, and so since last academic year we have gone from one to four English specialists, meaning that children aged six months to three years listen to and live in English and Catalan most of the hours they spend at school.

The specialists communicate with children all day long: when they arrive and we welcome them in the classroom, when we play, when we go outside to the playground, when we set the table for lunch, when we eat lunch, when we wash our hands, when we go to bed and get up, when we tell stories, when we suggest a variety of activities... We don't want to 'teach' English but instead live and communicate with each other in English just as we do in Spanish and Catalan.

Routines, which are repeated day after day, are particularly good times to learn an additional language. Repetition, the use of songs or rhymes and scaffolding are the resources that we teachers who speak English use. And, in fact, they are the same tools that any schoolteacher uses to communicate in their native language. The children aged 0 to 3 are learning not only English but also Catalan and Spanish, and therefore the strategies used to communicate and teach the language are the same in all the different languages we speak at school.

Through the ToWe Project, we have created our own materials that help us work with children at a higher standard. On the one hand, we have published a series of books for children aged six months to three years in which there are two main characters that go through situations very similar to the ones that the children at Petita Escola experience: going to the park, snack time, Christmas, bedtime, and so on. The simple illustrations and the texts that go with them, along with the fact that all the specialists tell the stories with the same words repeatedly throughout the year, makes them yet another tool to motivate the children with knowledge of a new language, while also expanding their vocabulary and allowing them to use it in everyday situations.

We have also developed a common glossary and songbook, which is still a work in progress. In this way, the entire English team shares the same foundation in vocabulary and songs.

The children's attitude towards English is completely normal. It is true that there is an adaptation period at the start of the academic year, just as there is with the spaces, the new faces, the pace and routines of school, but the children soon understand us and act according to what we are saying to them. Sharing time and space with teachers who speak their native language helps the children associate what each teacher is saying, and they also get used to understanding by drawing from non-verbal language, the context, and so on. Even though few of them speak to us in English fluently, many children, especially after the age of two, sing the songs with us and repeat words.

It was surprising to see how the majority of the children reacted during the job shadowing in Barcelona. Many of them spoke to the Norwegian or English teachers in English, and they sang them the songs that we sing in English.

We are convinced and pleased to see how the children at school are capable of understanding a language different to the one they speak at home and to enjoy an entire new world of songs, traditions and stories associated with that language, which will also become a basic tool for their learning and communication in the future.

Conclusion

The focus placed on toddlers' languages in this chapter responds to the belief that the manner in which languages (and communication) are used and promoted in the settings will clearly impact toddlers' and their families' and practitioners' wellbeing. Hearing their home language at the setting, seeing how it is made visible and how it is embraced by the adults around them gives toddlers a sense of self-esteem and respect for their identity, which is at the basis of quality provision. Furthermore, finding a coherent and appropriate way to approximate toddlers to new languages and cultures may also be the starting point for the global, sensitive citizen of the future. Therefore, the prime aim of bringing languages to the setting is not related to actually learning the language but rather to developing a certain attitude towards languages and cultures: 'Language learning in kindergarten and primary school is effective, for it is here that key attitudes towards other languages and cultures are formed and foundations for later language learning are laid' (European Commission, 2006). Working towards the development of positive attitudes towards language and language learning is vital to ensure a positive and effective learning process as toddlers grow older.

References

Brinton, D.M. (2001) 'The use of media in language teaching.' In Celce-Murcia, M. *Teaching English as a Second or Foreign Language.* 3rd Edition. Boston, MA: Heinle and Heinle.

European Commission (2006) *Promoting Language Learning and Linguistic Diversity: An Action Plan 2004–2006.* Accessed 12 September 2017 at http://eur-lex.europa.eu/legal-content/EN/TXT/?uri=CELEX:52003DC0449

Flores, C. and Corcoll, C. (2008) *Learning a foreign language in infant school: A challenge for the school.* Accessed 12 September 2017 at http://srvcnpbs.xtec.cat/cirel/cirel/docs/pdf/challenge.pdf

Flores, C. and Corcoll, C. (2011) 'Developing O'CLILS with very young learners.' *APAC Magazine 72,* 54–63.

Mistry, M. and Sood, K. (2015) *English as an Additional Language in the Early Years.* London: David Fulton.

Paniagua, G. and Palacios, J. (2005) *Educación infantil. Respuesta educativa a la diversidad.* Madrid: Alianza Editorial.

Siraj-Blatchford, I. and Clarke, P. (2011) *Supporting Identity, Diversity and Language in the Early Years.* Maidenhead: Open University Press.

UNICEF UK (1989) *A summary of the UN Convention on the Rights of the Child.* Accessed 1 February 2016 at https://www.unicef.org.uk/wp-content/uploads/2010/05/UNCRC_summary-1.pdf

CHAPTER 8

MEALTIMES

Àngels Geis

'Every child has the right to the best possible health. Governments must provide good quality health care, clean water, nutritious food, and a clean environment and education on health and well-being so that children can stay healthy. Richer countries must help poorer countries achieve this.'

(UNICEF UK, 1989, Article 24)

Lunchtime at school and setting

Mealtime is a part of what we call the midday break. This break also includes what the children do after eating and before starting the afternoon session. We believe that everything that happens every day is a learning opportunity, so everything that happens at a school or setting is a learning possibility. In this chapter, we will discuss the pedagogy of everyday life, meant as the part that revolves around the importance and high educational potential of situations that usually happen any day, situations in which there are both toddlers and adults. These actions range from classroom situations to playground time, clean-up, outings, mealtimes, entering and leaving school or setting and rest periods.

In the most relevant literature, we can find many references that uphold the high educational value of the everyday moments at nursery school or setting (Bassedas, Huguet and Solé, 1996; Bondioli and Nigito, 2011; Bosch, 2003; Casals and Defis, 1999; Domènech, 2009; Duart, 1999; Falk, 2004; Goldschmied, 1998; Hoyuelos, 2004; Jubete, 2007; Malaguzzi, 2001; Palacios and Paniagua, 2005; Ritscher, 2011; Ritscher and Staccioli, 2006; Silveira, 2002;

Van Manen, 1998, 2003). All the references highlight the goal of valuing all the moments that children experience together at school (all situations and sites of clean-up, meals, rest, play and entering and leaving school) as situations that are just as educationally important as those that the educator prepares as specific situations to work on the curriculum (interest centres, projects, corners, programming units, workshops, etc.).

⚙ REFLECTION 8.1

» Do you think it is important for the early years team to reach agreements on the role of the educator during times when the toddlers are cleaning up and during mealtimes at school or setting? Why?

» Do you hold any kind of meeting between early years practitioners and teachers (EYPTs) (key person or group tutors) and the kitchen staff and midday break monitors?

» Does your curriculum describe the functioning and pedagogical importance of mealtime at school or setting?

School and setting dining rooms and areas viewed as educational spaces

'The entire time that the children spend at school and at mealtime, are important moments, in the children's everyday lives.'

(Ritscher, 2011, p.120)

Eating not only contributes to helping the toddler grow physiologically, but it also helps them grow socially and affectively, culturally and intellectually. Anthropologists (Contreras and Gracia Arnaiz, 2005) assert that in almost all societies, the act of eating is a social activity. In fact, every culture has its own eating patterns, and this is why we talk about food cultures. According to Contreras and Gracia Arnaiz (2005), the eating behaviour of the majority of people can be predicted by their cultural patterns (technological resources, social organisation, activities, timetables, professions, family relations, responsibilities, etc.).

The fact that food is laden with cultural patterns leads us to think that we cannot apply or transplant models of how school or setting dining rooms or areas work in other cultures or from one culture to another, and instead that each school must clearly understand the cultural pattern that pervades their dining room or area.

If food plays such an important role in the process of people's enculturation, it is justifiable and valuable to analyse what we are fostering in mealtimes at school and settings.

We should consider contributions from psychology, such as the ones by Vendrell (cited in Anguera *et al.,* 2013) where she notes that bearing each toddler's needs in mind, the early ages are when we should strive to ensure a sound affective bond, emotional stability and health, stable behavioural patterns grounded in communication and peaceful coexistence. Therefore, not just any place or any way or any company is appropriate for mealtime. From the same field, Di Scala[1] stresses the cultural and inter-subjective dimension of human eating and its practices; she analyses how processes, symbolisation and cultural transmission occur among nursery school children and teachers during mealtimes (in this case breakfast).

In the field of pedagogy and school organisation, some authors (Díez de Andino and Cusachs, 2011; Escola Municipal Arc Iris, 2001) stress the need for each dining room plan to develop recommendations on the optimal functioning of the school dining room in conjunction with the school's administrative team and the coordinators of the team of dining room monitors. Within these recommendations, we find it fascinating that the authors note how it is important to ensure the right toddler-to-adult ratio, environmental conditions (noise, lighting, ventilation, size of the furniture), dealings with the staff and rules that make it possible to manage mealtime and determine how children can gain autonomy (Antón, 2007; Falk, 2004).

Pedagogues like Goldschmied (1998), Falk (2001), Ritscher (2011) and Ritscher and Staccioli (2006) respond to what mealtime should be like and what we can do at school or setting to improve it.

---

1   Maria Di Scala is an educational psychologist with a PhD in psychology from the University of Buenos Aires. Her doctoral thesis, Processes of Symbolisation and Food Practices at School, highlights the socialisation and communication possibilities of merienda (lunchtime) at nursery school.

REFLECTION 8.2

» What cultural patterns do you convey during mealtimes at your school or setting?

» Do you foster any kind of social habits (saying 'bon appétit', thanking the person serving you, etc.)?

» Do you work on environmental awareness and the responsible use of food in any way (such as by avoiding throwing out food and reusing leftover food)?

» What does having a healthy meal at school or setting mean to you?

A quality dining room or area for toddlers

Lunchtime should be a pleasant, calm moment for everyone (toddlers and adults), and for this to happen certain conditions must be in place, as explained above. Now we shall further flesh them out so they can become the focal point or horizon towards which we can focus our efforts at improvement. The requirements that should be borne in mind are varied: some refer to the place where the meals are held, the furniture and the tableware used, or the environment (noise, lighting or ventilation). Others refer to the way the diners are treated, that is, how their requests are dealt with, or how their eating speed or communicative needs are met. The third group refers to the possibilities that mealtimes afford for children to grow by developing their autonomy, or the way they are allowed to participate or to decide with whom to eat and how much food they want.

The dining room or area: place and time of communication

Toddlers take advantage of times that they gather with their peers to share experiences. We believe it is necessary for children to have a place during the midday break where they can interact with whomever they want and therefore decide with whom to talk and with whom to sit at lunch, share toys or experiences, and so on. Surprisingly, this does not happen at all schools or settings; in some the place and the classmate with whom they sit at mealtime is determined by the adult. Mealtime for a toddler, too, is best experienced in company, calmly, with the security that the adult or adults with them will tend to their needs, that they can speak with whomever they want, cordially and without the need to raise their voices, and receive encouraging messages from the adults or their peers. Mealtime is preceded by an explanation and a 'bon appétit'; it is a time when adults become referents of a proper tone of voice and good manners, and where no one is humiliated because they eat at a different speed. It should be a pleasant time with no uproar. These are the requirements we need for the school or setting dining room or area to foster good communication amongst peers and with the adults.

Therefore, ensuring that communication during mealtime is positively educational largely depends on the role of the adult. We adults have to know how to listen empathetically and how to engage in dialogues that make affective relationships possible. Furthermore, these dialogues should come with attentive looks, taking advantage of the importance of mealtimes as times of forging closer relationships. Nor should we forget that the way we address the toddler, our body language, can make it possible to establish even better bonds with the toddler, or can create distances. The early years teachers' role or style is the key, especially their communicative style. We must bear in mind the right voice expressiveness or modulation, the time we give the toddler to let them speak, stimulation of expression more than correction and the kinds of messages given (greetings, descriptions, orders, punishment, encouragement, etc.).

Regarding peer-to-peer communication, we believe that certain conditions must be in place for toddlers to be able to speak with each other. First of all, they have to be allowed to speak, but they also have to be beside a peer with whom they want to speak, which translates, as mentioned above, into their being able to choose where to sit and with whom to sit. Ultimately, the surrounding noise level must also allow for conversation. This communication is essential to the development of all toddlers. Malaguzzi reminds us of this when he says:

> The interaction among children has a fundamental value in the experience of the first few years of life. It is a demand, a desire, a need that all children have and that they want to meet in appropriate situations that foster this interaction. (Malaguzzi, 2001, p.58)

Therefore, the dining room is a place of relations, a time that can become the optimal opportunity to share and speak with each other. It is true that communication is impossible without someone else, yet it is also impossible without time. Daily life at school or settings should have a well-organised routine based on toddlers' – not adults' – needs. It should also be flexible enough so that toddlers can gather with their peers without being hurried. In short, it should be a daily routine that allows them to live their childhood.

During mealtimes, adults must respect toddlers' speeds, without this in any way meaning unnecessarily stretching out the time allotted for lunch. Properly regulating speeds also requires adults to prevent toddlers from waiting unnecessarily, either because they have to wait in the dining room or area, or because they have to wait until all or almost all the diners have finished their meal. The adult becomes a stable point of emotional reference who should give each child the security they need.

Therefore, mealtime should make dialogue and communication possible, and it should become a space where adults listen, explain when needed, follow models of good manners and ensure an organisation that allows toddlers to choose with whom they sit, even if not every single day. It should be a lunch without yelling, a time that helps the toddler get to know themselves, to become secure with their environments, to establish solid bonds with adults and peers, a dining room where they can experience and practise respect for others. In short, mealtime should be a time of wellbeing and enjoyment.

⟳ REFLECTION 8.3

»   Do you like to speak comfortably with your friends when you go to a restaurant or attend a celebration?

»   Can the children do the same at lunchtime at their school or setting?

Educating children's autonomy in the dining room or area

The school or setting should become a space of culture, of challenges that make it possible for toddlers to grow, and a place where we must trust toddlers and provide them with autonomy so that they can construct their own cognitive processes. This process has no timetables, nor can it be limited to interest centres or specific topics; instead, it is part of the everyday experiences, challenges and actions in which toddlers engage.

Both mealtime and clean-up before and after lunch should be a time in which toddlers participate. This means that they can help to set the table with the tablecloth, dishes, cups, cutlery and some of the additional items, such as water pitchers or bread, as well as actions like getting soap, washing and rinsing off their hands and going to the bathroom. When lunch is finished, each toddler should be able to put their dishes, cutlery, napkins and cups into the right tubs, as well as remove rubbish and place it in the right receptacle. Clearly, the utensils used should make it easy for the toddler to do as much as they are capable of doing for themselves.

By this we mean that all toddlers should feel useful, but more importantly they should know that there are actions in their daily lives that they have to do for themselves, because they can and because they are learning how to be responsible for the things that they use. These actions – setting and clearing the table or taking care of their own cleanliness – not only empower toddlers to be more autonomous, they also help boost their self-esteem. Obviously, engaging in this kind of participation requires organisation of the space, certain materials and utensils, as well as organisation of the time and the tasks. It is essential to think about a strategic place to put the tubs to collect the tableware, the way the adults should supervise each situation and how the table setting should be organised.

In the process of growth and the acquisition of autonomy, mealtimes are also when each toddler gets to know themselves, to learn about their tastes, whether they eat a lot or a little and what they need in order to care for their bodies. This learning is intrinsically associated with the adult's respect for the toddler, which means that each toddler should eat depending on how hungry they are, and that each should be able to serve themselves their own food or, if this is not possible, serve themselves something like bread, water, salad or dessert.

In order for the dining room or area to become a space that educates the toddler to become more autonomous, it is essential to allow them to participate in each of the tasks, to ask them questions and tend to their needs, and to have adults who are capable of listening, watching and respecting their speeds.

♻ REFLECTION 8.4

Children aged two often tell us, 'No! Not you! I want to do it by myself!' because they want to and can do many things by themselves:

» Do you keep this in mind at mealtimes?

» Can they set the table?

» Can they decide how much they eat?

» Can they help put things away afterwards?

» Are they allowed to serve any dishes?

The dining room or area: educational space and materials

> Eating well is not only a question of food but also a question of context. (Ritscher and Staccioli, 2006, p.51)

In virtually all cultures, celebrations such as birthday parties, weddings or gatherings of friends revolve around a table. In these cases, the act of eating is an intimate, family-oriented time. In contrast, at school or setting it becomes an act carried out publicly in a space designed for this purpose.

School is a place of encounters and relations where toddlers should find pleasant spaces with stimulating materials, along with documentation that shows us how to make a school or setting and how to understand the spaces, learning and life that happen there. The spaces should help generate good relations and friendliness. We believe that any space, and specifically the dining room or place where meals are held, should not only meet physiological needs but also should foster the overall development of those who use it. It should convey the culture of the context and provide affective security. Regarding the place where meals are held, Goldschmied (1998) says that we all want it to smell pleasant, for the food to be displayed nicely, for people to tend to us attentively and for the atmosphere to be relaxed, without either pressure or noise. Ultimately, it should have a *family* feel.[2]

---

2   Claus Jensen, a Danish pedagogue, describes that the space at school becomes family-like if we incorporate elements like the ones we find at home. For the dining room, this would include a tablecloth, napkins, dishes, cups, etc. This information is from a conference 'Les relacions i l'ambient físic' (the realtionships and the physical environment) presented by Claus Jensen 2 March 2013 at Municipal Theater of Sant Feliu de Guixols.

♻ REFLECTION 8.5

> » How do you set the table when you have guests and want them to feel good?

> » How do we set the table so that children feel good in the school dining room?

EYPTs' experiences, reflections and strategies from England, Norway and Spain

ENGLAND

Janette Barber from Heathfield Children's Centre, Achieving for Children, Twickenham, London

This chapter has boosted our knowledge and understanding of 'wellbeing at mealtimes'. For example, a student practitioner was preparing to be observed and positioned herself at the 'snack table' to support children's learning such as, using spoons to scoop and serve food. The tutor said 'snack table isn't an activity' and rejected it, not appreciating the educational content within. We have used the ToWe Project to focus on mealtimes to highlight to all staff, students, volunteers and particularly parents the importance of snack time as both an opportunity to support children's learning *and* their wellbeing – demonstrating that learning and wellbeing are intrinsically linked.

We used audits to establish a 'snack café' that is predictable and promotes independence with adult support. We provide special cups, for example, that allow children to see the tipping point. The café is still a work in progress, for example, toddlers can't reach fruit in the middle of the table which is something which we need to address, and some practitioners require food hygiene training, but with continued reflections on our practice we are developing further.

Video

Filming allowed us to watch families at the snack café and assess what was going well or needed improvement. Observations highlighted that, without staff input and modelling, parents seldom talked to children or responded to children's protests and insisted that they eat. Children were taking too much food and wasting it. Children were not practising feeding themselves or drinking from an open cup. I asked one parent, 'If you didn't feed...would he feed himself?' She said, 'Yes but he makes a mess.' I said, 'Let him, he's learning.' When children can feed themselves, they are better equipped to cope during mealtimes at nursery and school. Children were not being taught to tidy away dishes, dirty toys were put on the snack table, some children climbed onto the table – all of which indicated that we needed to find out more about family mealtime routines.

Practitioner

Practitioner support isn't always available at the snack table; however, filming showed that adults are our greatest asset – encouraging children to have a go at practising skills and demonstrating the 'hand over hand' technique and crucially modelling effective practice to parents/carers and other volunteers and students.

Practitioners encouraged talk among peers and adults, 'Do you want some apple? Red or green?' They used children's first names: 'Let's give ...a share', encouraging conversations about family mealtimes and children's experiences. One mother said that in her culture mealtimes are 'not for talking', however she now encourages talking at mealtimes, the only time in the day when the family comes together.

Fussy eaters

Parents report that mealtimes can be stressful. If fussy eaters want to taste food it's important that practitioners support this 'Wow! Moment' and in that instance do not insist on 'wash hands first' policy, as this can be distracting. We signpost parents in such cases to health professionals, cooking and messy play activities. Parents now report that exploring food with no pressure of eating has helped children to relax around food. We carefully manage these activities to support children and parents to find them enjoyable.

Tablemats

Visual learning prompts on the wall and handouts were not as effective as we had intended. So we redesigned the tablemats to include learning prompts such as, 'Teach us to feed ourselves', '...drink from an open cup', and so on. We included guidance and the developmental age that children acquire feeding skills. We included Makaton signs such as 'finished', and pictures and labels of fruit and vegetables. This has proven successful in supporting toddlers' independence skills and related wellbeing, with children talking about the pictures and parents reading the prompts.

They also requested tablemats to take home which will support the impact on the home learning environment. We are developing these in the home language of families attending, to ensure that they feel included.

Parents'/toddlers' voice

We investigated the impact that snack café was having with 34 families. Six parents reported feeding concerns. Sixteen parents were surprised at what their toddler could do independently. Twenty-three parents are allowing their child more independence at family mealtimes. By highlighting the learning intentions more parents are letting their toddlers feed themselves and drink from open cups.

NORWAY

Harrieth Elin Kristiansen Strøm from Sandvedhaugen Barnehage, Sandnes Kommune, Sandnes

Meals in toddler groups

It is perhaps during mealtimes that we can document the most measurable changes before and after the ToWe Project. During our first meeting in Kingston, the project group watched a video of a mealtime in a pre-school setting in Barcelona. It made an impression on us. We watched toddlers who were allowed to be independent, make their own decisions, collect their own food, tidy up after themselves, talk to each other during the meal without excessive adult control and decide where they wanted to sit at the table. We saw that these children mastered far more skills relating to the meal situation than we allowed our children to. We became very aware that major changes are both necessary and appropriate in this regard.

So, the next question was: How can we bring this about?

The ToWe Project manual and tools and strategies within the book provided us with an excellent and specific professional tool for a new approach to mealtimes. We started well, with some good theory about focusing on quality in everyday situations at the start of the manual. We started to look more closely at how our daily routines could include learning opportunities. As mentioned previously, we started with mealtimes, but the professional awareness we focused on during the meal situation soon had an effect on other daily routines as well, such as the cloakroom situation. (The cloakroom situation is a daily routine in which children dress for outdoor play and undress afterwards.)

We followed the plan we had agreed on for implementing the theory and change in practice, which had already been decided within the project group. During the process, we came up with some focus words. These included: sense of mastery, independence, communication, learning, enjoyment, influence, self-realisation and *wellbeing*.

The staff from the various groups discussed how we could achieve the objectives and concluded that the key reason we saw so little independence, for example, was down to us – the adults. We needed to have far greater faith in the children being able to do what they wanted and a stronger belief that their wellbeing would improve if they were simply allowed to experiment.

We have paid little attention to some of the more practical aspects of the assessment tool. For example, we may well want lower tables and chairs, so that the younger children do not need to be lifted up onto the chairs, making it easier for the children to collect things they need during the meal, but this was not possible, so we did not focus on this. Other things such as tablecloths and serviettes are also not important to us in this context.

The children were given responsibility for collecting cups, plates, butter knives and lunch boxes. They were each given their own place at the table and they could choose who they wanted to sit next to. During the meal, they were given much more freedom as regards what topping they wanted, whether they wanted butter on their bread or what they wanted to drink, for example. We saw that the children became more independent, far more aware of other children around the table, and more inclined to help each other. If the children forgot anything when they set the table, they were allowed to get down from their chair and collect what they needed.

The communication between the children around the table increased. We adults played a more withdrawn role and focused more on supporting the children's communication. We undoubtedly became much better at watching the activities unfold around the table, such as play, enjoyment and wellbeing, instead of noise and bad manners. The children also tidied up after themselves with their own cloth and looked at themselves in the mirror when washing after each meal. The children also became more involved in preparing food, laying the table and sweeping up afterwards.

We adults saw the sense of mastery in the faces and eyes of the children and we saw the joy. We also saw that the children wanted to become far more involved in other everyday situations. We adults became more playful in our communication with the children. We observed more and were able to support the children more easily when they needed it. We saw that their wellbeing improved.

The parents also saw that the children learned new skills and wanted to 'do things themselves' at home too. It was a fantastic start to the ToWe Project and there was considerable engagement amongst the children, staff and parents. When the children from the ToWe Project groups moved up to the larger group of three- to five-year-olds a few months after we had started the meals in the toddler group, they became known as the ToWe children in the larger group, because of the skills they had learned, the positive interaction between them and the wellbeing that the staff saw.

SPAIN

Mireia Miralpeix Anglerill and Mª Àngels Domènech Pou from Mas Balmanya Escola Bressol Pública, Surara Serveis, Cataluña

As an important 'educational time', mealtime has always been at the forefront of our educational project. Before starting to participate in the ToWe Project, the entire team had already reflected on mealtime, and there had been previous efforts that had led to different changes.

After reading the materials, each of us filled out the grid of good practices. This is when we realised that we still had a long way to go and a lot to reflect on if we wanted to foster children's independence at mealtimes to the utmost.

Along the way, we have had to deal with the resistance that we ourselves have put up, such as deciding that we couldn't offer the children more independence when serving themselves and removing their dishes from the table because the dining area is very small and did not allow it.

When based on our reflection on the content of the ToWe Project handbook and books tools and strategies, we were able to realise that 'fostering children's autonomy during mealtimes' is a goal we wanted to achieve, so we began to search for the way to do it, and we found it. We realised that in order to make something possible, the first step is believing and trusting that it is possible, and that whatever we decide will be impossible will be.

'Whether you think you can or think you can't – you're right.'

Henry Ford (1863–1947) quoted in Tschannen-Moran and MacFarlane (2011)

Based on this 'change in attitude' in the team, we began to 'make changes to the space and materials'. We laid out the tables in such a way that the children could get up to get their dish from the table. We also changed the tableware they use with smaller dishes, so that small trays with food could be placed in the middle of the table, and the cutlery was also smaller so that they could serve themselves as much food as they wanted. This also allowed us to place a pitcher of water, bread and all the condiments on the table permanently so that the children could get them whenever they wanted.

In this way, all the reflections that translated into 'We can't do that because we have no space' turned into, 'What do we have to do to let the children do this?' And this is how this year mealtime has become a 'pleasant, autonomous space of social interaction', a place where the children enjoy this time shared with their peers and adults.

References

Anguera, M., Geis, A., Vendrell, R., Iglésias, J. and Cuenca, N. (2013) *Com han de menjar els infants i els adolescents: Aspectes psicosocials i nutricionals de l'alimentació*. Lleida: Pagès.

Antón, M. (2007) *Planificar la etapa 0–6. Compromiso de sus agentes y practica cotidiana*. Barcelona: Graó.

Bassedas, E., Huguet, T. and Solé, I. (1996) *Aprendre i ensenyar a l'educació infantil*. Barcelona: Graó.

Bondioli, A. and Nigito, G. (2011) *Tiempos, espacios y grupos: El análisis y la evaluación de la organización en la escuela infantil: DAVOPSI*. Barcelona: Graó.

Bosch, E. (2003) *Educació i vida quotidiana: Històries breus de llarga durada*. Vic: Eumo.

Casals Grané, E. and Defis, O. (1999) *Educación infantil y valores*. Bilbao: Desclée De Brouwer.

Contreras, J. and Gracia Arnaiz, M. (2005) *Alimentación y cultura: Perspectivas antropológicas*. Barcelona: Ariel.

Díez de Andino, C. and Cusachs, N. (2011) 'El menjador, part del projecte educatiu d'una escola.' *Infància, 178*, 27–32.

Domènech, J. (2009) *Elogi de l'educació lenta*. Barcelona: Graó.

Duart, J.M. (1999) *La organización ética de la escuela y la transmisión de valores*. Barcelona: Paidós.

Escola Municipal Arc Iris (2001) 'Temps de migdia al parvulari. At the ICE of the UAB, Els reptes de l'educació infantil.' *V Jornades d'innovació en l'etapa d'Educació Infantil*. Bellaterra: Universitat Autònoma de Barcelona, 187–190.

Falk, J. (2001) *Menjar*. Barcelona: Rosa Sensat.

Falk, J. (2004) *La conquesta de l'autonomia*. Barcelona: Rosa Sensat.

Goldschmied, E. (1998) *Educar l'infant a l'escola bressol*. Barcelona: Rosa Sensat.

Hoyuelos, A. (2004) *La ética en el pensamiento y obra pedagógica de Loris Malaguzzi*. Barcelona: Octaedro.

Jubete, M. (2007) *El valor educatiu de les coses de cada dia*. Barcelona: Graó.

Malaguzzi, L. (2001) *La educación infantil en Reggio Emilia*. Barcelona: Octaedro.

Palacios, J. and Paniagua, G. (2005) *Educación infantil. Respuesta educativa a la diversidad.* Madrid: Alianza Editorial.

Ritscher, P. (2011) *Slow school. Pedagogia del quotidiano.* Firenze: Giunti.

Ritscher, P. and Staccioli, G. (2006) *Viure l'escola.* Barcelona: A.M. Rosa Sensat.

Silveira, M.C. (2002) *Rutines, activitat a l'escola.* Barcelona: Graó.

Tschannen-Moran, M. and MacFarlane, B. (2011) 'I know I can!' In Lapp, D. and Fisher, D. (eds.) *Handbook of Research on Teaching the English Language Arts.* London: Routledge.

UNICEF UK (1989) *A summary of the UN Convention on the Rights of the Child.* Accessed 1 February 2016 at https://www.unicef.org.uk/wp-content/uploads/2010/05/UNCRC_summary-1.pdf

Van Manen, M. (1998) *El tacto en la enseñanza.* Barcelona: Paidós.

Van Manen, M. (2003) *El tono en la enseñanza. El lenguaje de la pedagogia.* Barcelona: Paidós.

CHAPTER 9

FUTURE VISION – WHAT NEXT?

Helen Sutherland and Yasmin Mukadam

'The foundations for virtually every aspect of human development – physical, intellectual and emotional – are laid in early childhood. What happens during these early years (starting in the womb) has lifelong effects on many aspects of health and well-being – from obesity, heart disease and mental health, to educational achievement and economic status.'

(Marmot, 2010)

Introduction

This chapter will explore the impact and value of the tools and strategies provided to support toddler wellbeing throughout this book and the ToWe Project. It will describe how the project has underpinned early years practitioners' and teachers' (EYPTs') understanding of supporting wellbeing, provision and improved overall practice through the use of the Toddlers' Wellbeing Framework and the four key pedagogical characteristics:

1. Read and research

2. Critical thinking

3. Reflective practice

4. Skills and attitudes

This chapter will also identify and discuss some of the results and impact from the research carried out during the ToWe Project (2015–2018) with the partner settings.

The findings and reflections from the project and this book provide a positive vision for looking forward and developing future provision and practice in driving forward EYPTs' continued abilities to support toddlers' wellbeing through engagement, empathy and encouragement.

The ToWe (Toddler Wellbeing) Project

The ToWe Project is an ERASMUS+ Key Action 2 School Education Strategic Partnership Project funded by the European Union and the British Council. The aims of the ToWe Project are:

> to improve the practice of early years practitioners working with disadvantaged toddlers, in order to help them get the best start to formal education, in the hope that they will go on to maximise their potential and be active citizens in the future. (Sutherland and Dracup-Jones, 2015, p.3)

The ToWe Project identified the following three European Union priorities of 'enhancing the quality of early childhood education and care, high quality learning opportunities and reducing disparities in learning outcomes affecting disadvantaged learners' (Sutherland and Dracup-Jones, 2015, p.3).

The ToWe Project provided the setting partners' EYPTs with a range of innovative learning opportunities and a holistic approach to support and maximise toddlers' wellbeing. Bespoke training materials and tools were presented at a five-day training event held at Kingston University for practitioners and teachers from the setting partners, to develop their knowledge, understanding and practice of supporting toddlers' wellbeing. EYPTs were able to maximise their continuous professional development (CPD) opportunities through planned job shadowing, where practitioners were able to reflect, discuss and share experiences and practice between England, Norway and Spain.

Toddlers' Wellbeing Framework

In Chapter 1, the 'Toddlers' Wellbeing Framework' and 'Four Pedagogical Characteristics' were introduced, to enable the development of EYPTs' own knowledge and understanding of toddlers' wellbeing, and how they can enhance their own development through these characteristics. The setting partners from the ToWe Project have successfully applied the 'Toddlers' Wellbeing Framework' and 'Four Pedagogical Characteristics' as seen in the 'EYPTs' experiences, reflections and strategies' within this and previous chapters. This has underpinned EYPTs in their implementation of the strategies and tools that have improved their provision and practice to enhance toddlers' progress and outcomes.

The skills and attitudes of empathise, engage and encourage have been used to support EYPTs in improving wellbeing within the setting through developing a better understanding of how to support toddlers' wellbeing and how to improve the provision and development of strategies through the use of reflection, discussion, critical thinking, reading and researching. This shared approach has supported setting partners as they have developed their practice to ensure consistency as a whole setting approach involving all members of staff.

♻ REFLECTION 9.1

What opportunities can be created within your setting using the Four Pedagogical Characteristics?

1. Read and research

2. Critical thinking

3. Reflective practice

4. Skills and attitudes:

   » Empathise

   » Engage

   » Encourage

How can these be used to develop, support and improve wellbeing within your setting?

What challenges might you face in implementing this framework?

What strategies and actions can you put in place to overcome these challenges?

ToWe Project research

The ToWe Project followed an interpretative qualitative paradigm with EYPTs applying an action research model of observe, reflect, act, evaluate and modify; to investigate, explore and evaluate their own practice and develop solutions and strategies to support and improve provision for disadvantaged toddlers. Following on from this, a Case Study Impact Report using case study methodology complementing the action research of the practitioners and teachers has enabled investigation of the impact of the project.

A mixed method approach was used to gather both qualitative and quantitative data through focus group interviews with each country's EYPTs, online reflective discussion fora, group reflective sessions and questionnaires. This was done to enable a shared ongoing reflection between EYPTs from all participating countries. These data-gathering strategies were integrated and interwoven into the project design from the outset and were carried out at key points within the project (Sutherland and Dracup-Jones, 2015).

Results and impact

Three focus groups were held with all the setting partners from the project with the use of semi-structured interview questions to aid the discussion and these identified key impacts to supporting toddlers' wellbeing through the development of practice and provision.

The key themes arising from focus group 1 were:

- recognition of good practice and areas for improvement

- sharing and reflecting on practice, development of staff knowledge and understanding of wellbeing

- modelling and sharing the importance of wellbeing with parents

- adapting the environment.

The key themes arising from focus group 2 were:

- mealtimes:
    - introduction of new resources to support toddlers independence
    - embedding snack café into the routine, focusing on reducing noise.
- wellbeing tools and strategies:
    - encouraging toddlers' autonomy
    - conveying the importance of wellbeing to parents.
- state of the art:
    - materials shared with colleagues to provide a collaborative approach in supporting toddler wellbeing
    - good feedback from colleagues to recommend changes to other settings
    - confidence and impetus of colleagues to change things and renew their focus on toddlers' wellbeing and resilience.
- challenges:
    - lack of funding, staffing and resources
    - introducing project to new staff and parents in a timely manner
    - keeping colleagues positive when settings are facing challenging times, such as, restructuring.

The key themes arising from focus group 3 were:

- positive comments from parents regarding new sessions
- ToWe Project materials informing practice being displayed
- parents wanting to take away materials to carry out at home to continue the 'play/do' together activities
- developed resources
- reaffirming what practitioners and teachers already do that benefit toddlers' wellbeing

- monthly meetings to share information and embed good practice, putting the toddler at the centre of provision, through the use of reflection

- comparing and contrasting other setting partner countries' practice, for example, standing back and recognising when to let the toddler persevere with a task and not intervening

- revisiting tools and strategies when working in different environments to make it more enabling for the toddlers and parents

- using knowledge gained from the ToWe Project to support new changes and challenges, for example, setting up new environments

- working together with their colleagues from the ToWe Project's setting partnership.

An initial example of the impact of the results and reflections has been identified from each partner country's focus groups:

Impact of the ToWe Project in England

An example of the impact of the project was the development and changes made to the snack time routine at the children's centres. Child-friendly serrated knives were purchased so that the toddlers could individually cut up their own fruit safely. EYPTs noted that the toddlers really enjoyed the snack time, as it promoted independence skills and learning opportunities.

Impact of the ToWe Project in Norway

An example of the impact of the project was that it was noted by the pre-school EYPTs that the toddlers moving up to the pre-school room were demonstrating good independence skills and confidence, as the children were asking where to dispose of the food waste after mealtimes. The pre-school staff started to call these children the 'ToWe children' 'because of the skills they had learned, the positive interaction between them and the wellbeing that the staff saw' (Harrieth Elin Kristiansen Strøm, Sandvedhaugen Barnehage, Norway, Chapter 8).

Impact of the ToWe Project in Spain

An example of the impact of the project was that through continuous reflection, entrenched practice and 'poor' habits were identified and discussed, recognising these attitudes and developing strategies to improve practice.

The skills and attitudes of 'empathise, engage and encourage' have been applied within these examples and show the impact of how they reflected on the situation, created a solution and supported the change to improve the situation.

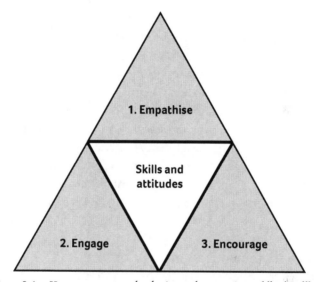

Figure 9.1 – Key components to developing and supporting toddlers' wellbeing (Sutherland and Mukadam, 2018)

⟳ REFLECTION 9.2

Identify and reflect on an area of practice to support toddler wellbeing that needs developing. How can the skills and attitudes of empathise, engage and encourage be applied to improve the area for development?

The dimensions within the toddler wellbeing framework have provided EYPTs with a flexible, holistic and adaptable approach to embedding and prioritising wellbeing within their setting.

EYPTs' experiences, reflections and strategies from England, Norway and Spain

ENGLAND
Alison McGee from Achieving for Children (Social Enterprise for Kingston and Richmond Children's Services) and Rachel Lazarides, Kew, Mortlake, Barnes and East Sheen Children's Centre Hub Manager, Achieving for Children, London

Achieving for Children (AfC) have valued the opportunity to be involved in the ToWe Project and have been excited about undertaking action research, learning from others through direct first-hand experiences about international perspectives on toddlers' wellbeing and ultimately considering 'How can we use this knowledge and experience to ensure that we are supporting our own toddlers' wellbeing across our settings?'

As dedicated professionals, we hold the belief that research *must* be used to inform and further develop practice and it is now our *duty* to share that more widely for the benefit of other toddlers across our settings.

The desire to learn from action research, and a commitment to do so, is an easy first step but that is not to say that there have not been certain challenges along the way. As I reflect upon the process so far I would like to share some of the success, but also some of the aspects from which we have learnt along our journey, and how we will use this to inform our next steps.

Ensuring a shared understanding from the start by 'lead practitioner' and setting manager

This is vital – as the project needs to be valued, with necessary time and effort required valued. In order for this to happen both the aim *and* the process need to be understood. Linked to this is the value of reflection as a tool, as it is not the audits and materials per se within the ToWe Project manual *but* the reflection, discussion and resulting impact which is crucial. Reflection as a professional development tool may not be as prevalent across settings in recent years; however, this has always been an effective part of early years practice.

Indeed, all children's centre and nursery activity must always be 'outcome focused', asking 'What is the impact for children and families?' 'How can we really be sure without such reflection on the different aspects of wellbeing?' Whether considering opportunities for child's voice or the effectiveness of interaction at snack time, the success of the ToWe Project is that it truly highlights this effective practice.

So what has worked well? We found that having a manager involved at all stages throughout the project – from initial focus planning, through to evaluation and summary reporting, and even being afforded the opportunity to undertake job shadowing – has been valuable and effective. Going forward, we are fortunate that we can share experiences from this managerial perspective which addresses the points made above (see Rachel Lazarides' reflection below).

Securing team involvement and support

If reflection then is at the heart of the ToWe Project, it is therefore essential for all the team to be 'on board'. What have we learnt during the project? That this aspect takes time, that there is a need for dedicated time to be allocated for all staff, including support staff, to be involved. It is insufficient for team members to be simply aware of the focus of particular areas throughout the ToWe Project; rather it is necessary that they are fully involved in both planning and reflection, particularly in relation to their own particular role in supporting toddler wellbeing. So asking again, what has worked? Regular team meetings have provided opportunities for update and discussion around the ToWe Project, sharing the impact on practice. We have found that it is helpful in terms of supporting shared understanding if a more 'tangible and concrete' area in relation to wellbeing is the starting point for team involvement. An example of this was the identification of toddlers' mealtimes as an agreed area on which to focus as all settings had an identified need for consistency of approach to snack/mealtimes. The concrete audit tool gave a starting point, which did aid initial discussion and supported full team involvement. As mentioned earlier, the challenge then going forward is to ensure that time is given for on-going reflection, resulting from use of the materials, and developed as an aspect of practice which continues to drive improvement.

The need for settings to have 'ownership' but also clarity of purpose and a plan of action

A quality of the ToWe Project is that it is not a set programme to follow or a series of tools to use, complete and tick off, which as I have alluded must be outlined and explained to ensure all settings appreciate. The fact that settings are able to use the tools and materials in a way and order which best suits the needs of their settings is an asset. However, two things which we have identified as essential are:

- The need for clear focus and planning by lead practitioner with advisor/setting manager support to ensure that the use of the materials and time for reflection and discussion *continues* to remain high focus.

- The need to link the ToWe Project to *existing* good practice and curricular areas. For example, practitioners may say 'supporting wellbeing is intrinsic to my role, being part of the Early Years Foundation Stage (EYFS) which underpins our practice' and, yes, this is true. The question is, therefore, how can the ToWe Project materials and tools help us to reflect on this and ensure that we truly *are* supporting toddler wellbeing?

Rachel Lazarides – reflections from a manager's perspective
Strategies developed and implemented to improve areas and practice:

- Giving practitioners increased opportunities to shadow, and observe the practice of others and themselves.

- Ensuring that concrete examples of good practice and understanding are highlighted and celebrated so that staff are feeling confident and positive when analysing their own practice.

- Using the 'mantle of the expert' to engage staff in self-reflection... and showing them that, as a manager, I value this.

Impact on the toddlers
Consistency is essential to wellbeing for young children. To achieve consistency between adults in a toddler's life is inherently beneficial to their wellbeing. Therefore all adults in the setting need to be involved in reflection on the impact of our practice for toddlers.

Impact and reflections on staff
The experience of job shadowing highlighted the importance of time for reflection, but also the value of having the opportunity to do this formally and informally. Audits and recording tools help to promote and give status to the process, however there needs to be capacity for individuals to have other informal and more frequent opportunities alongside these: simply sharing ideas over lunch, or going for a walk to think, so that reflection becomes embedded and intrinsic to everyday delivery.

Impact and reflections on parents

In contrast to nurseries parents stay with their children when attending the children's centre, therefore there is scope to involve them as practitioners, and encourage them to reflect on how they support their child's wellbeing. This has the potential to impact long term. Parenting courses provide an environment in which parents are encouraged to reflect on their practice, and share useful tools. The team can consider ways to extend this and create similar safe opportunities for sharing and reflection within Stay and Play sessions, perhaps evaluating sessions collectively, or one-to-one when updating a child's learning journey.

NORWAY

Ingrid Eikeland Andersen from Sandvedhaugen Barnehage, Sandnes Kommune, Sandnes

Since Sandvedhaugen kindergarten was established in 2008, we have had a special focus on the role of adults, as we believe this is vital for the quality that each individual child encounters. For example, we have taken part in a project concerning values, where we studied the adult's mediation of values. Through the ToWe Project, we have gained a stronger belief that the adult's attitudes and organisational approach can improve wellbeing and support the development of all children.

Clear tools have been and can be useful in the continuation of our ToWe Project. Specific tools help us to reflect and bring about shared attitudes with regards to how we as teachers should safeguard the children's wellbeing and development. Clear and specific tools also help us to pass on ToWe to new employees and unskilled co-workers to enable them to better understand goals and methods. The tools can contribute to quality assurance if the adults are willing and able to understand.

We will continue the work to enable children to become independent and master routine situations. Being a playing adult is of great importance for the children's wellbeing in these situations.

The attachment theories of Bowlby will be a fundamental aspect and will be used during the familiarisation period, for example. We will involve guardians to an even greater extent than before and sharpen the tasks and role of the key contacts during the familiarisation period. The agenda for parents' meetings with new parents has been altered since we joined the ToWe Project.

We will also take with us the important and essential cooperation which the kindergarten should have with the child's home. We will look in more detail at the child's home arena and dare to ask questions which we did not dare ask before. We now see the value of the contribution that a greater understanding of the child's home situation can make to a better and more targeted organisation in the setting.

Through secondments (job shadowing) in Barcelona and London, we have discovered that we can learn a lot from kindergartens which are essentially different from ourselves. This difference enhances our ability to reflect on and improve our own practice. Our awareness of our own practice increased when we had to explain to others why we chose the educational approach and practice that we did.

We will advance many specific ideas that the ToWe Project has given us. However, last but not least, it is about the attitudes of the adults. Reflection and observation are excellent methods for arriving at good forms of communication, both with individual children or with the group of children as a whole.

We are continuing with a new project, 'The development supports kindergarten'. For this project, we will draw on the experience which we have gained through the ToWe Project. The experience of being observed by external parties will benefit us, as it is part of the set-up that the adults will be observed in teams. Again, a focus will be placed on the role of adult and its importance for the wellbeing and development of the children.

SPAIN

Natàlia Turmo and Sílvia Turmo from Petita Escola, Barcelona, Cataluña

The ToWe Project began as a project with a start and end date. We soon realised that the ToWe Project did not end with the project; instead, it is a way of doing things and a way of being, a way of viewing early childhood education, a conception of children, and a way of working. Petita Escola will forever be a ToWe school and we have internalised a way of working that we will not abandon.

This way of doing things and working consists of placing children at the heart of our questions, decisions and actions. Why do we do what we do? Is it good for the children to do it this way? What's the goal? Does it bring wellbeing to children, their families and the team of professionals?

At Petita Escola, we are used to recording and observing ourselves and questioning what we do, how we do it and why we do it. Taking snippets from our day-to-day lives and conflictive moments, and analysing how we can improve wellbeing have become the way we work thanks to the ToWe Project.

ToWe has led us to rethink our day-to-day work and to delve to the essence of our jobs, which is none other than the children's wellbeing. But it has also led us to redefine ourselves as a school by rewriting our objectives, values and foundations. This has led us to change spaces and materials, as well as attitudes.

While reading the theoretical handbooks (ToWe Project manuals, tools and audits) that the university experts had developed, we felt it was a perfect description of the essence of early childhood education; all of us teachers and all our colleagues participating in the project from other schools were in complete agreement on this. We felt that the handbooks expressed precisely what we believed, the reason we go to work every day. The surprise comes when you question yourself, watch yourself work, record yourself and evaluate yourself. That is when you realise that the theory in which you believe does not always emerge in day-to-day practice, and that often practice, routine and poor habits become entrenched and are difficult to detect and especially to change. This is one of the most important lessons we learned with the ToWe Project: how easy it is to reorganise a classroom, add or change furniture, materials, resources... and how complicated it is to recognise attitudes that could be improved and, once they have been recognised, to actually change them! This is a long-term undertaking, one that never ends...a process of constant individual and team improvement, always with the children at the core.

One of the points that ToWe has made easier for us, which will be difficult to continue, is the possibility of sharing experiences with professionals from other countries. This sharing, contrasting, questioning and comparing is so enriching that we will try to continue engaging in similar experiences.

Watching how our job is done internationally at centres that share the same essential values has helped us open up our perspectives, situate ourselves on a blank page and be able to take decisions without prejudices, without letting ourselves be swayed by what we were used to doing, or what the families expected of us, but instead **thinking** (and we write thinking in bold) about what will be best for the children and having checked this and debated it with other professionals with a variety of vantage points.

However, it won't be so difficult for us to continue the job shadowing in Spain. We have already begun to visit other centres in Catalonia and have learned a lot.

The future is more ToWe, more wellbeing, more job shadowing. We have to spread this self-reflective, self-critical way of working based on self-observation, self-evaluation and constant exchange to other centres in order to seek improvements centred on the children's wellbeing.

The future vision for enhancing the quality of toddler wellbeing

The future vision for enhancing the quality and opportunities for toddler wellbeing needs to be fully embraced by all staff if this is to be successfully implemented within the setting. The wellbeing of toddlers also needs to be valued and understood by other stakeholders and policy makers. UNICEF (2007) and the UK government, All Party Parliamentary Group on Wellbeing Economics (2014) have recognised the need to support wellbeing through recommendations and government interventions. Therefore the tools and strategies from this book and the ToWe Project enhance and complement the need for prioritising wellbeing within early years settings. Bringing parents 'on board' and supporting their understanding of wellbeing and how to engage with their toddler can have a long-term positive impact on the toddler, as parents are encouraged to reflect on their role and engagement with their toddler.

Going forward it is important that the tools and strategies within the book are not meant as a set programme and a prescriptive package, but are to be used as a flexible and holistic approach that can be adapted to meet the needs of the toddlers within the setting. This aids EYPTs in developing their knowledge and understanding of wellbeing, providing them with a toolkit of strategies that enable them to be reflective, inspired and innovators of practice.

EYPTs can develop this further through sharing experiences and reflecting continually on practice and provision. By developing a collaborative working approach EYPTs can enrich their understanding and enhance their perspectives as they learn from other teachers and practitioners. Figure 9.2 shows possible links that can be established to enable collaborative working in the future.

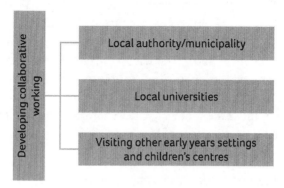

Figure 9.2 – Developing collaborative working

One of the benefits of working collaboratively with other countries is that EYPTs can learn from each other, gaining an international perspective of engaging and supporting toddlers learning. The British Council offers e-twinning: this link provides access to twinning with European early years settings https://www.britishcouncil.org/etwinning. Other European countries will have their own version of e-twinning.

⟳ REFLECTION 9.3

Looking at Figure 9.2 - Developing collaborative working:

» What opportunities does your local authority, community or municipality have to work collaboratively with your setting?

» What other types of settings might be useful for staff to visit? For example:

  – Forest School approach

  – Children's centres

» Where is your nearest university?

  – How might you be able to work with them on future projects and research?

Conclusion

The vision for the future is how the tools and strategies from this book and the ToWe Project can be used and embraced by EYPTs to enable reflective, inspired and innovative practice within their setting.

It is important that EYPTs create an open dialogue of reflective sharing, experience and expertise to develop their pedagogical knowledge and understanding and to inform and improve their own and others' practice and provision in supporting toddlers' wellbeing. This is important as the toddler's experience has a lasting impact upon their wellbeing (Department of Health, 2014). The dimensions within the toddler wellbeing framework of:

- family, home and environmental factors

- health of toddlers

- setting environments

- development and learning

- voices and expressions

- early languages

- mealtimes

are set out to support and improve the wellbeing outcomes for toddlers within each of the chapters within this book.

Wellbeing continues to be a critical and current area of focus for governments, members of the Organisation for Economic Co-operation and Development (OECD) and UNICEF. The UNICEF current Report Card 14, (UNICEF, 2017) aims to 'ensure healthy lives and promote wellbeing for all at all ages' (Goal 3) as a clear target by 2030.

> Every high income country invests in its children: healthy, educated children are better able to fulfil their potential and contribute to society. By contrast, problems of child development often carry through into adulthood, with the resulting social costs accruing to the next generation. (UNICEF, 2017, p.4)

This reiterates and reinforces the importance of supporting toddler wellbeing as a continued area that will impact upon EYPTs and toddlers into the future.

References

All Party Parliamentary Group on Wellbeing Economics (2014) *Wellbeing in four policy areas*. Accessed 21 November 2016 at http://b.3cdn.net/nefoundation/ccdf9782b6d8700f7c_lcm6i2ed7.pdf

All Party Parliamentary Group on Wellbeing Economics (2015) *Mindful Nation UK Report by the Mindfulness All-Party Parliamentary Group (MAPPG)*. Accessed 21 November 2016 at www.themindfulnessinitiative.org.uk/images/reports/Mindfulness-APPG-Report_Mindful-Nation-UK_Oct2015.pdf

Department of Health (2014) *Wellbeing: Why it matters to health policy*. Accessed 3 October 2017 at https://www.gov.uk/government/uploads/system/uploads/attachment_data/file/277566/Narrative__January_2014_.pdf

Marmot, M. (2010) *Strategic Review of Health Inequalities in England Post-2010. Fair Society, Healthy Lives: The Marmot Review Executive Summary*. Accessed 29 January 2018 at www.parliament.uk/documents/fair-society-healthy-lives-full-report.pdf

Sutherland, H. and Dracup-Jones, K. (2015) *Enhancing the Education and Wellbeing of Disadvantaged Toddlers through the Development of Training and Materials to Support Early Years Practitioners (Grant Application)*. ERASMUS+, Key Action 2, School Education Strategic Partnership Project. [2015-1-UK01-013431]

ToWe Project (2015–2018) *Enhancing the Education and Wellbeing of Disadvantaged Toddlers through the Development of Training and Materials to Support Early Years Practitioners*. ERASMUS+, Key Action 2, School Education Strategic Partnership Project. [2015-1-UK01-013431] Accessed 2 November 2016 at www.toddlerswellbeing.eu

Sutherland, H. and Mukadam, Y. (2018) *Toddlers' Wellbeing Manual*. ToWe Project 2015–2018. Accessed 1 December 2017 at www.toddlerswellbeing.eu

UNICEF (2007) *Report Card 7: Child poverty in perspective: An overview of child well-being in rich countries* Accessed 2 November 2016 at www.unicef.org/media/files/ChildPovertyReport.pdf

UNICEF (2017) *Report Card 14: Building the Future Children and the Sustainable Development Goals in Rich Countries*. Accessed 3 October 2017 at https://www.unicef-irc.org/publications/pdf/RC14_eng.pdf

Index